I0502464

WONDER DROSS

BY
JAMIE ARMES

COPYRIGHT © 2016 JAMIE ARMES
ALL RIGHTS RESERVED.

ISBN-13:
978-1542484091

ISBN-10:
154248409X

This book is printed one sided
for a few reasons.

You can color in the pages
if you like.

Or maybe you don't want to.
It's okay to just look.

Or maybe you want to tear
pages out and hang them
on your fridge.

That's okay too.

Point is, you've got options.

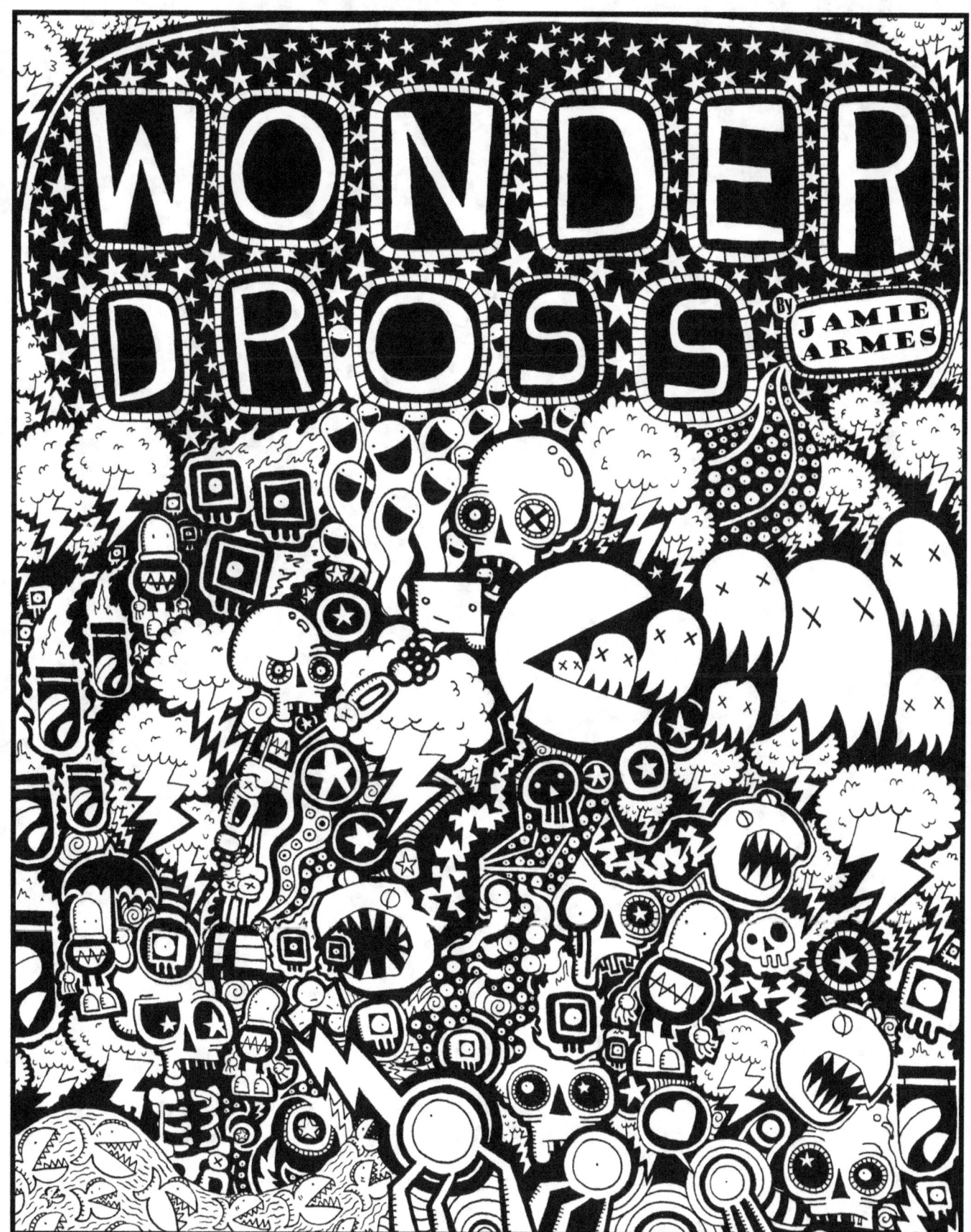

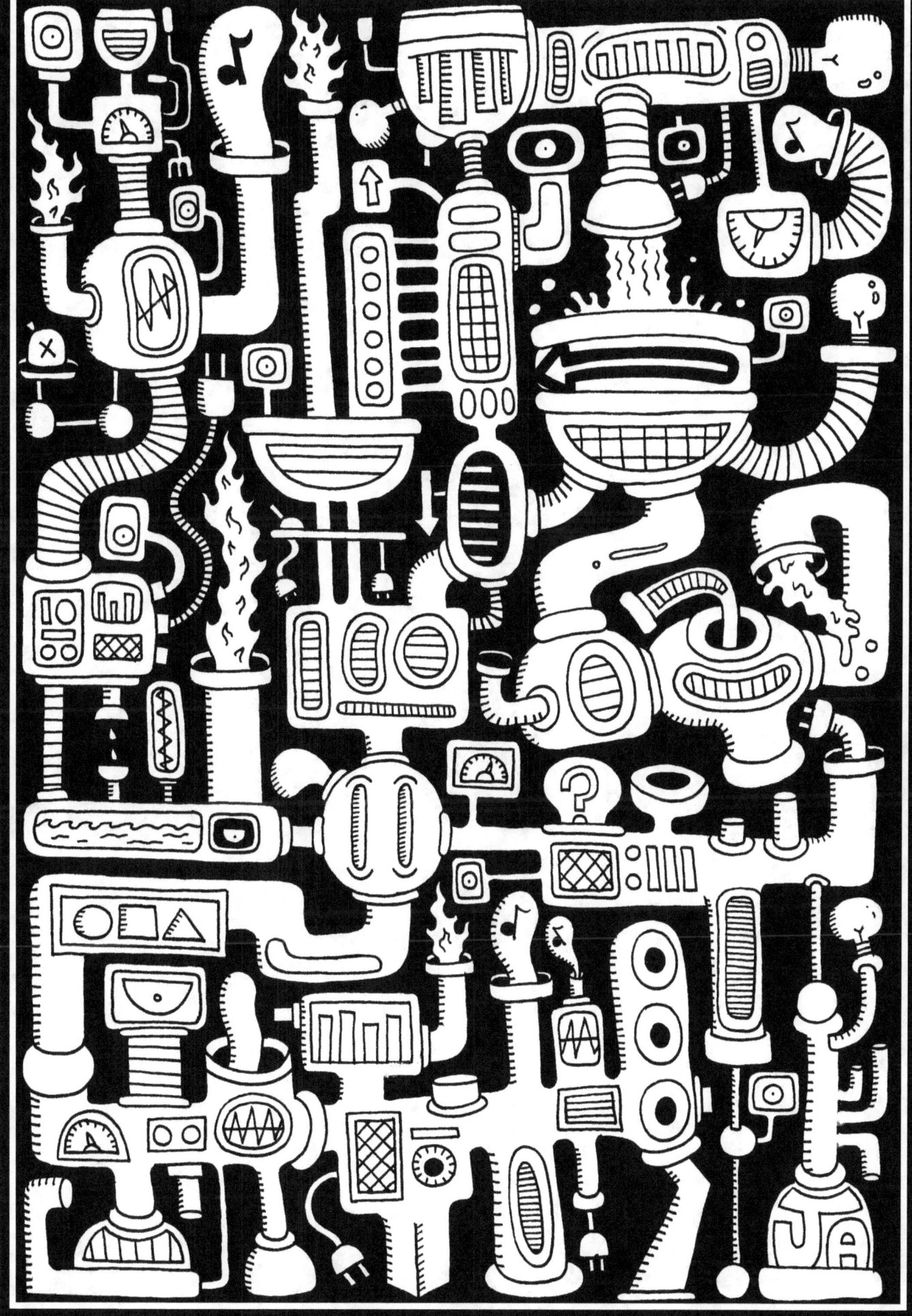

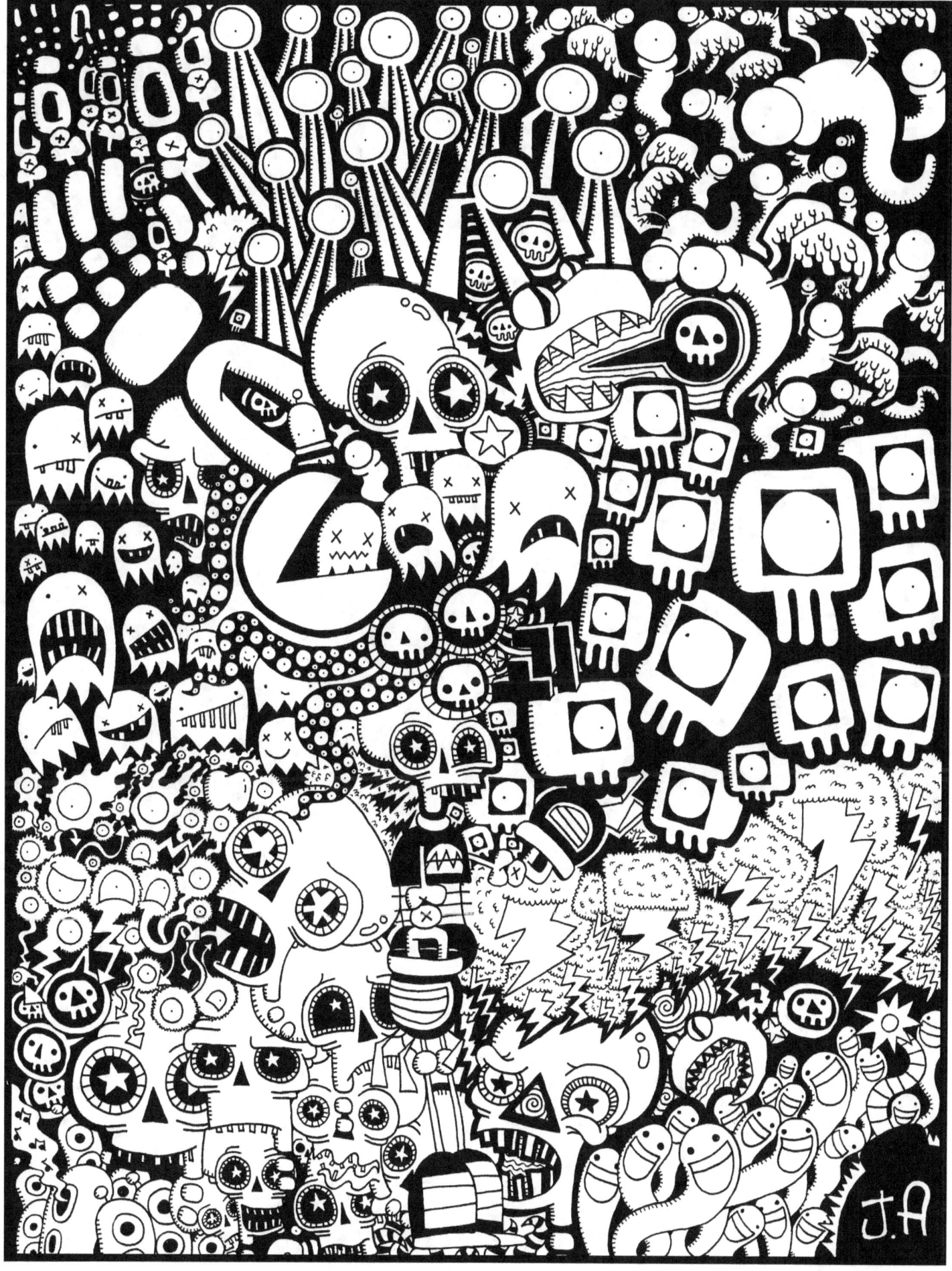

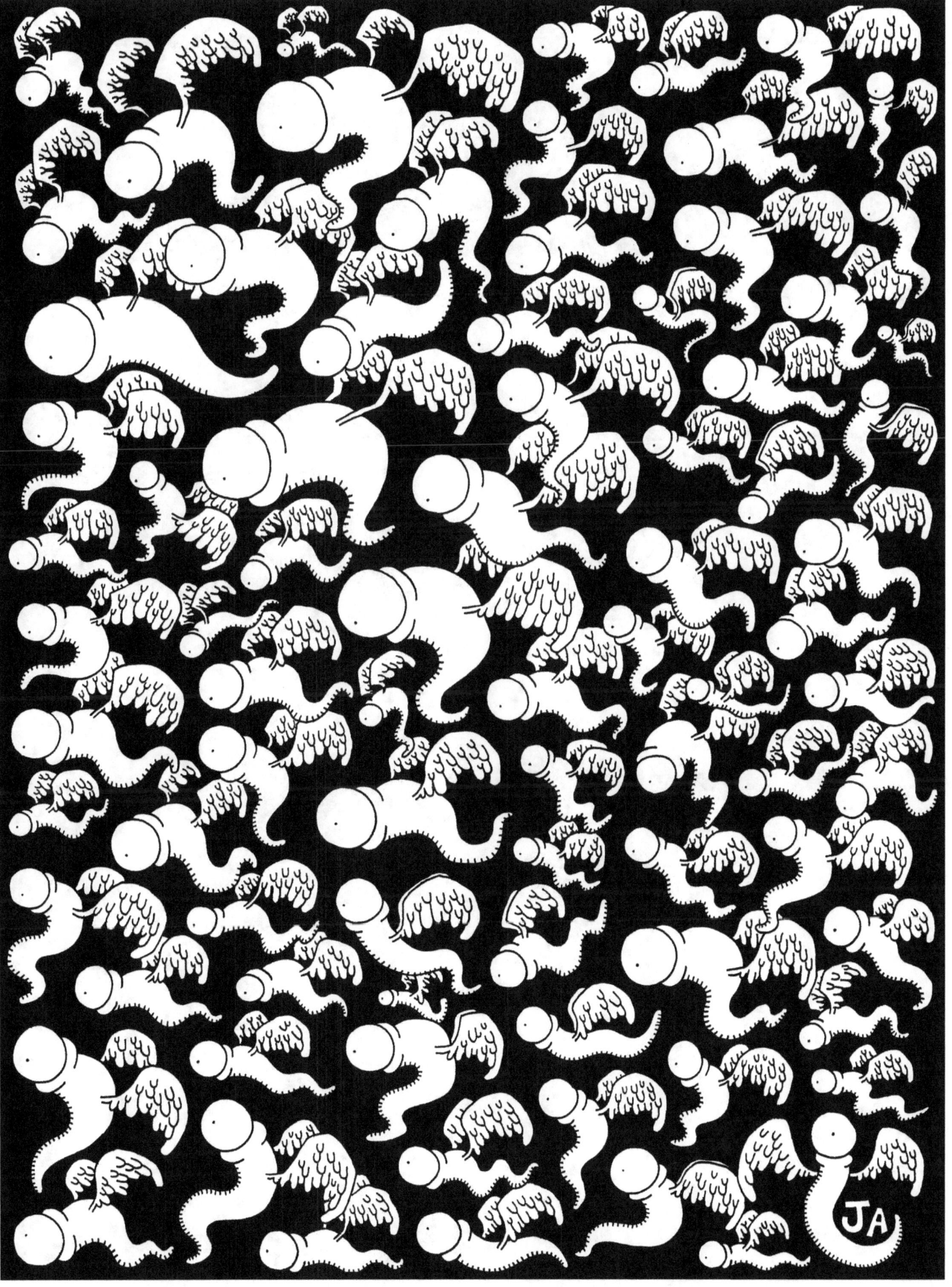

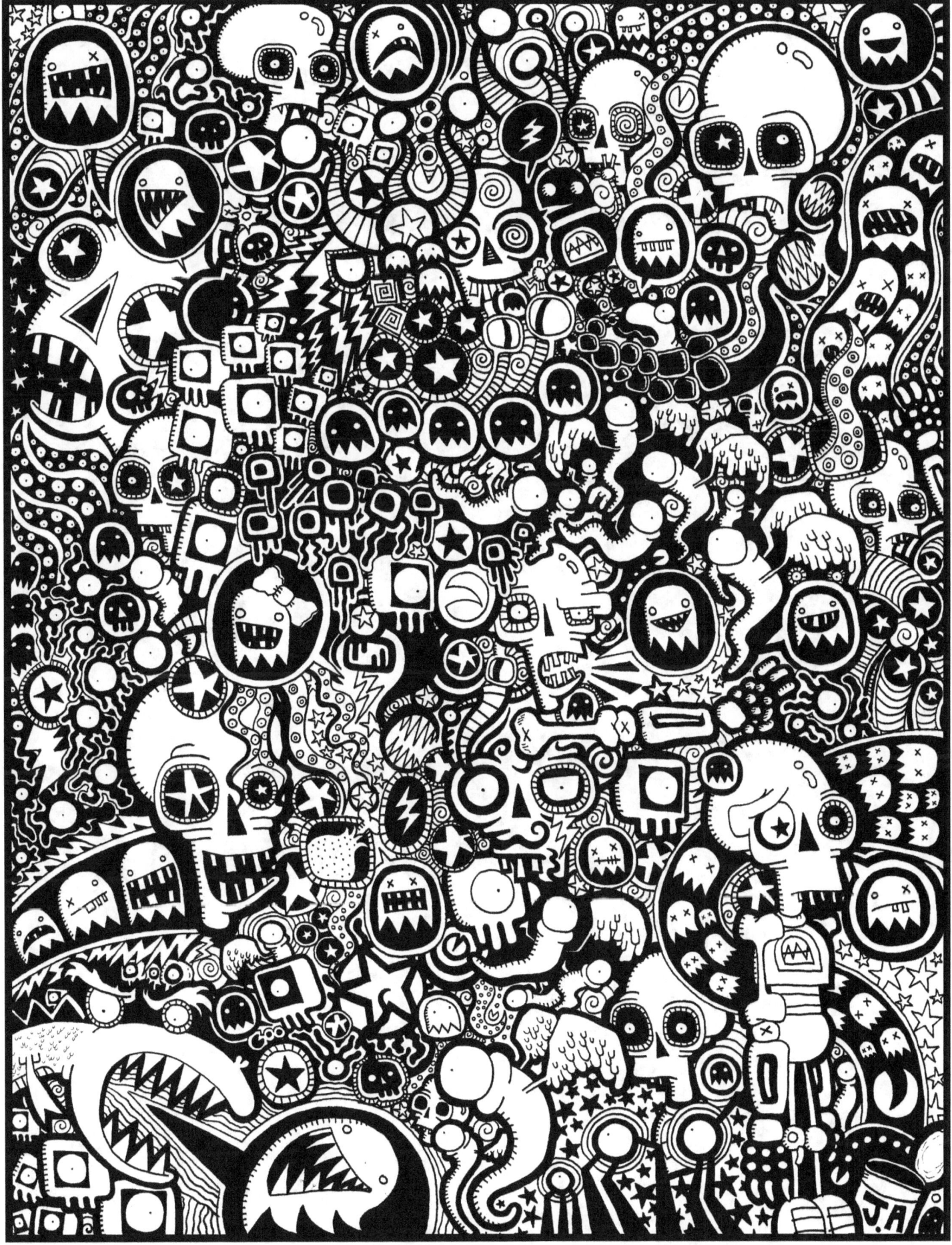

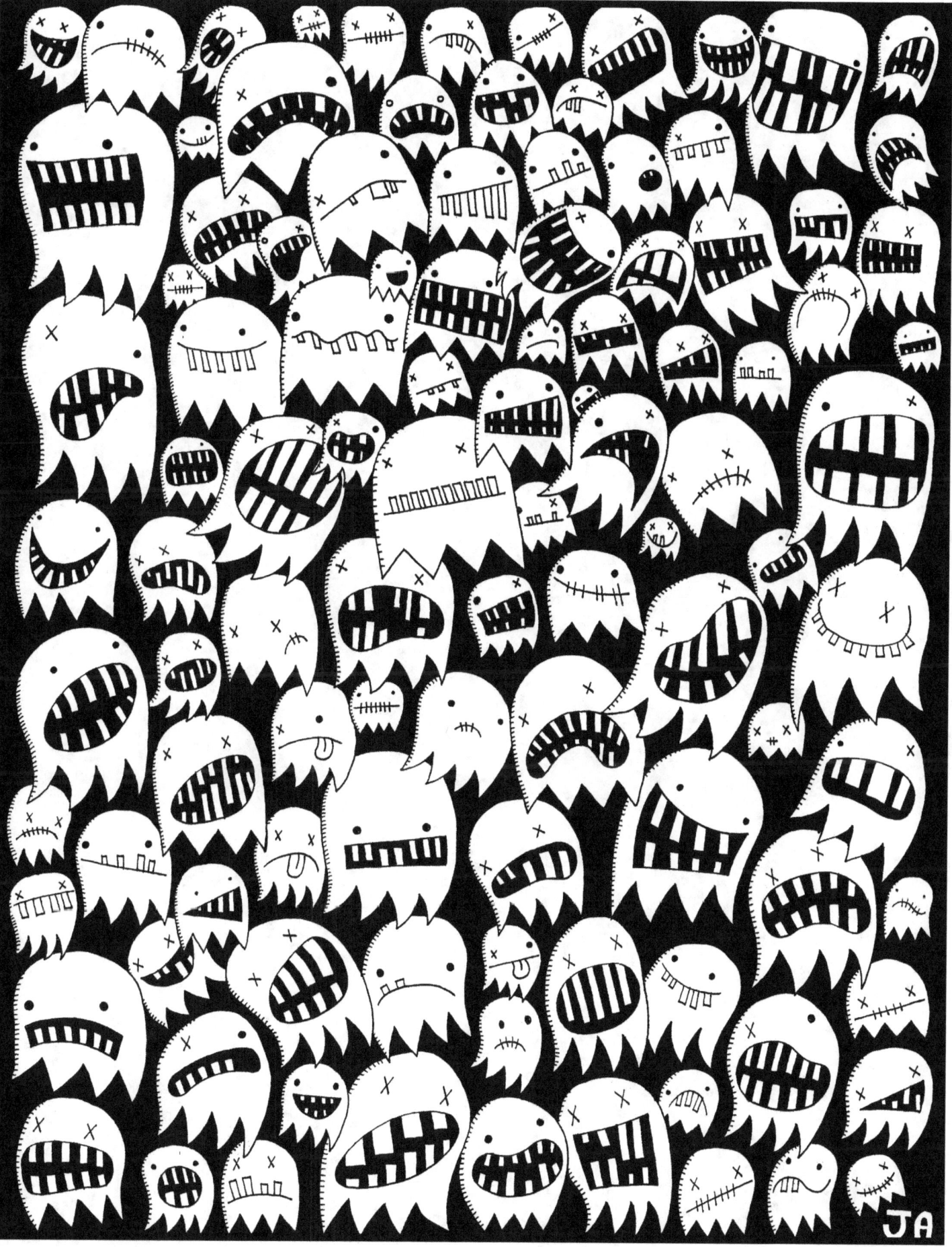

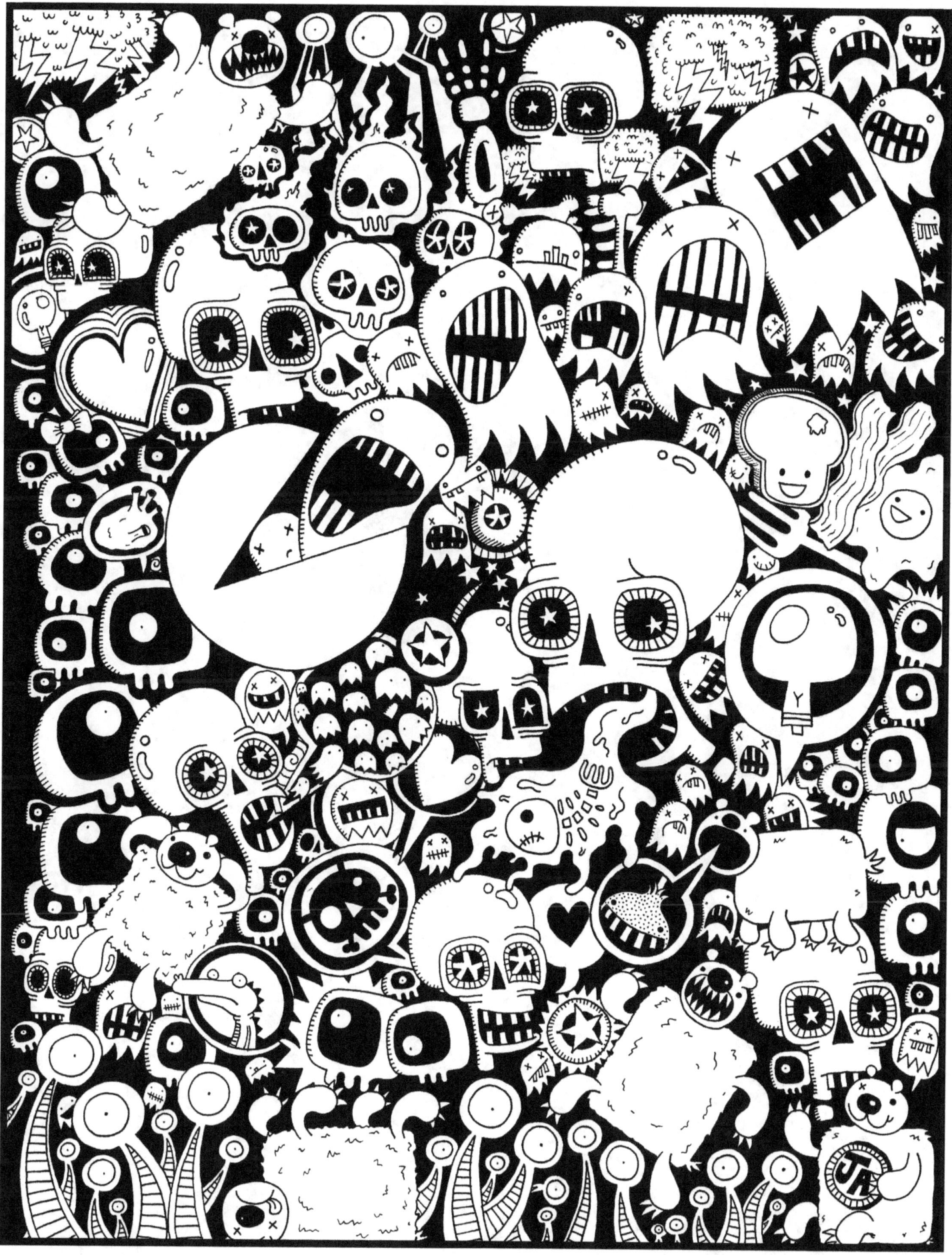

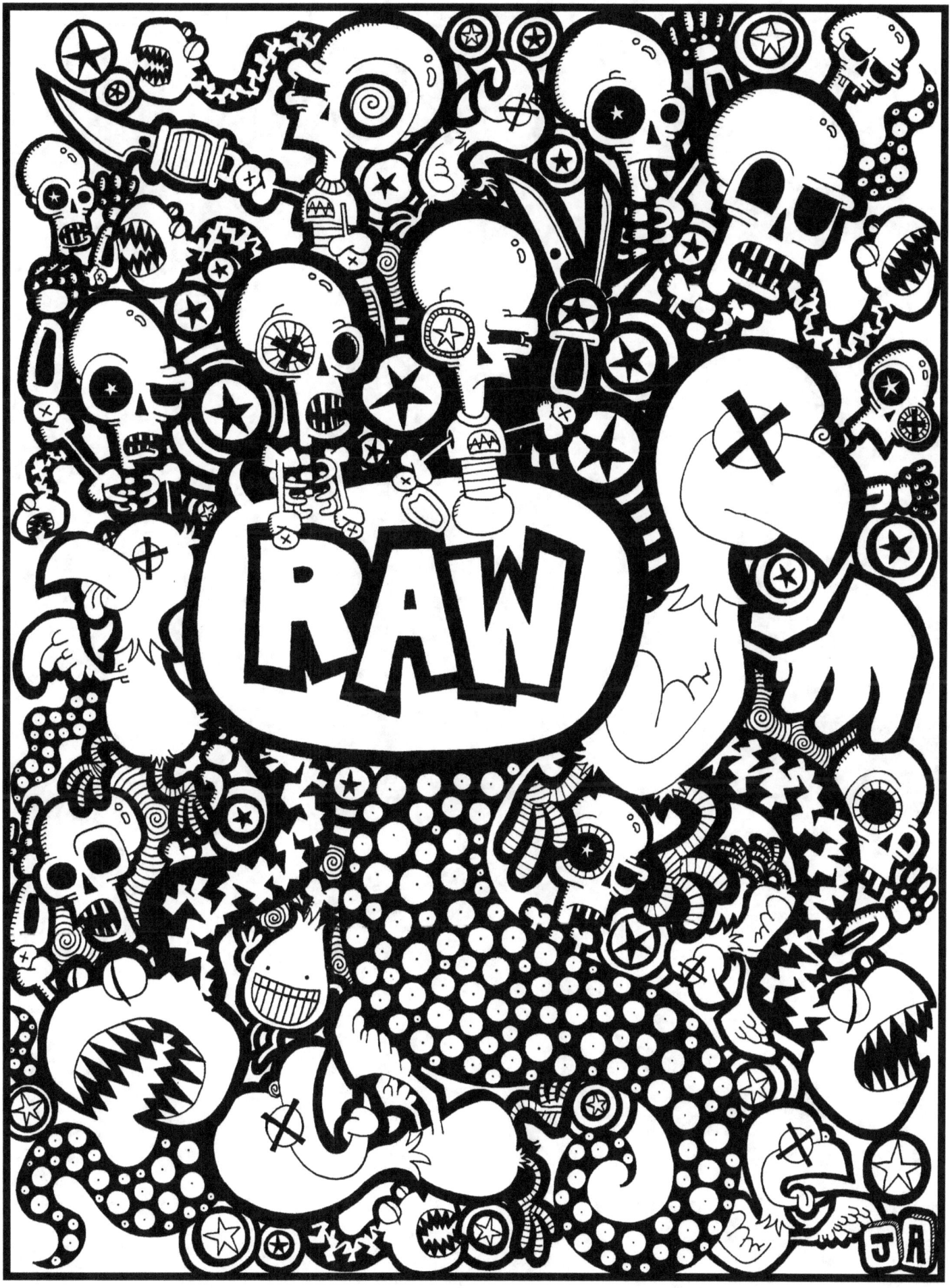

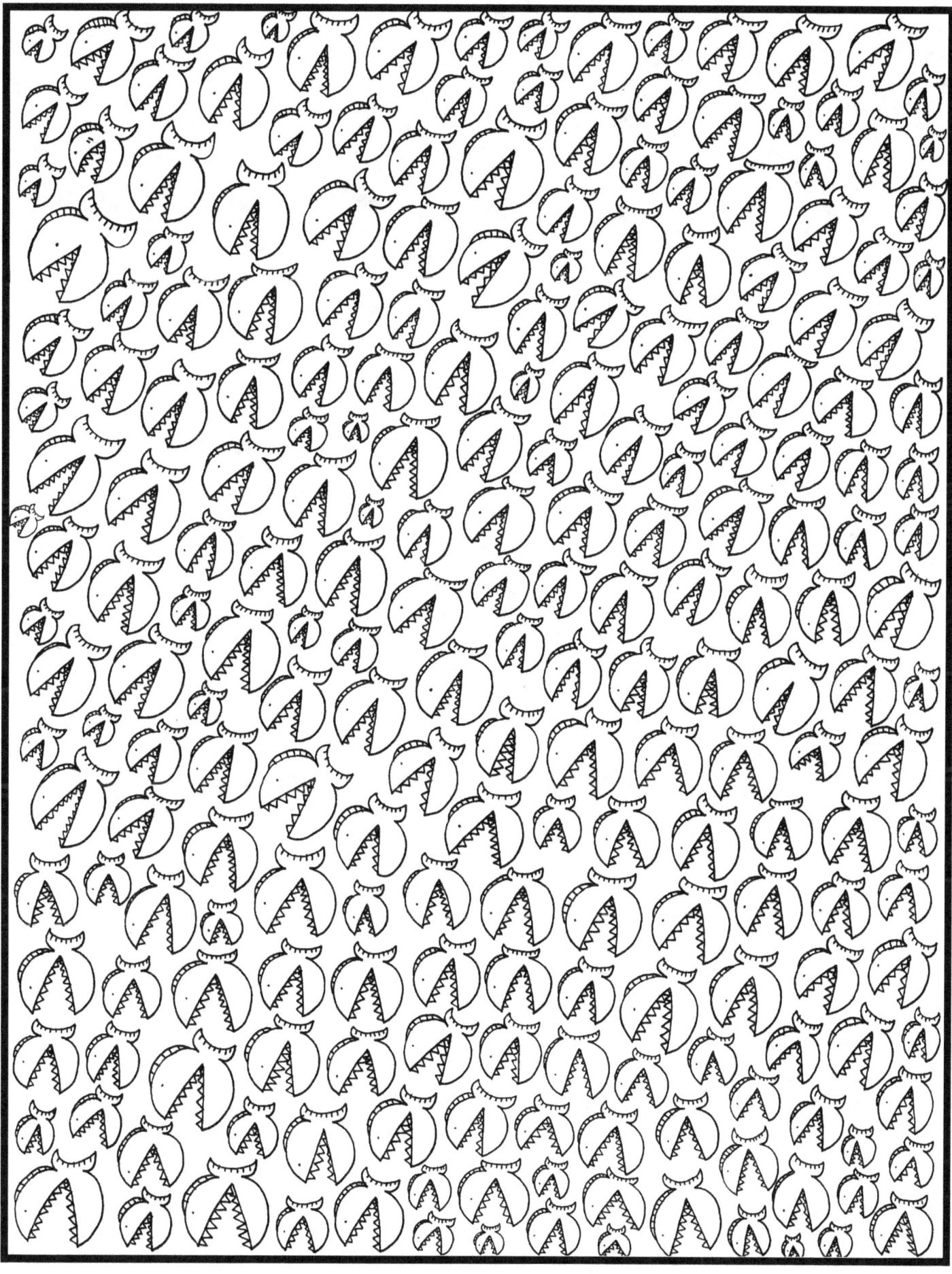

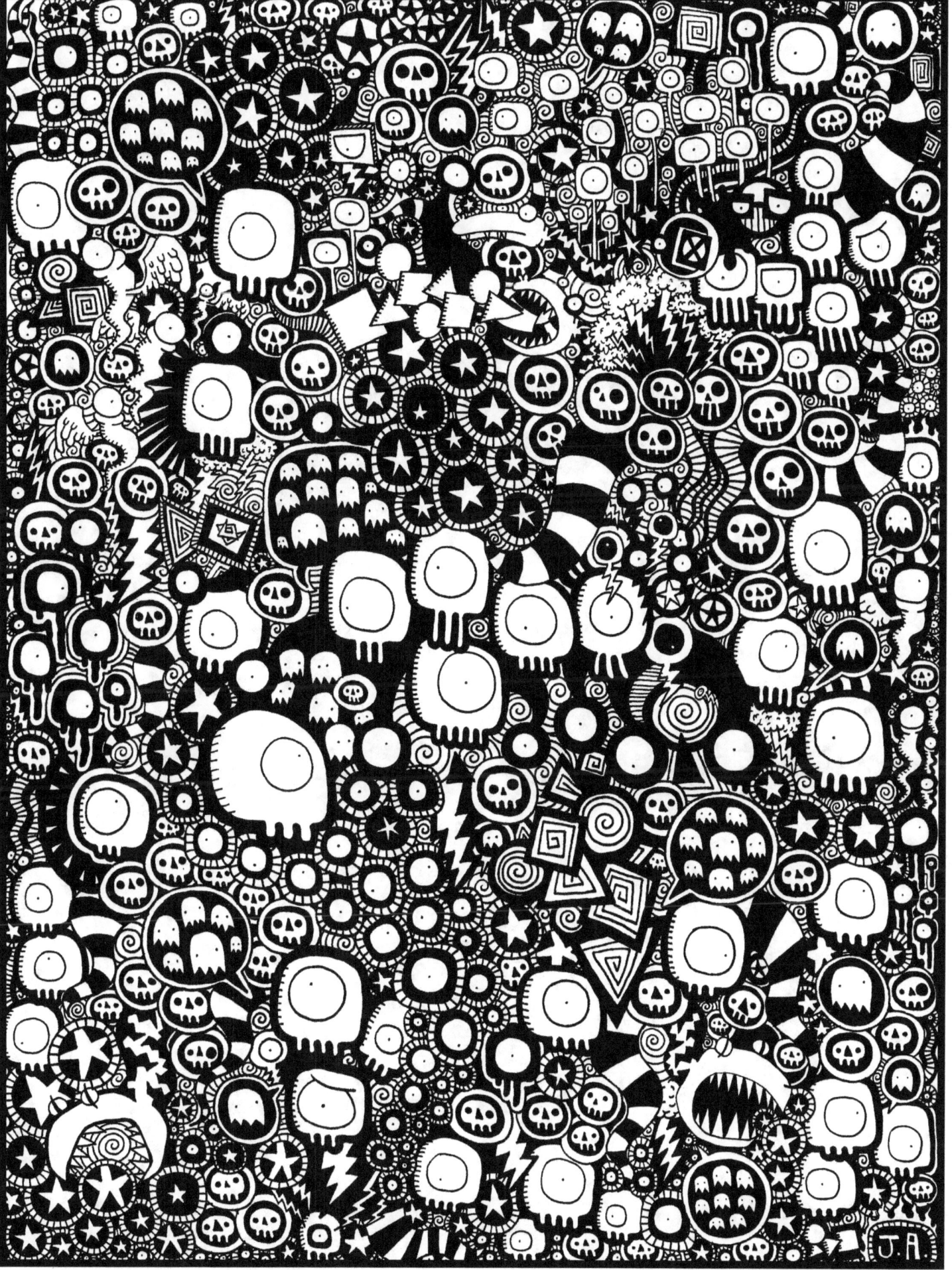

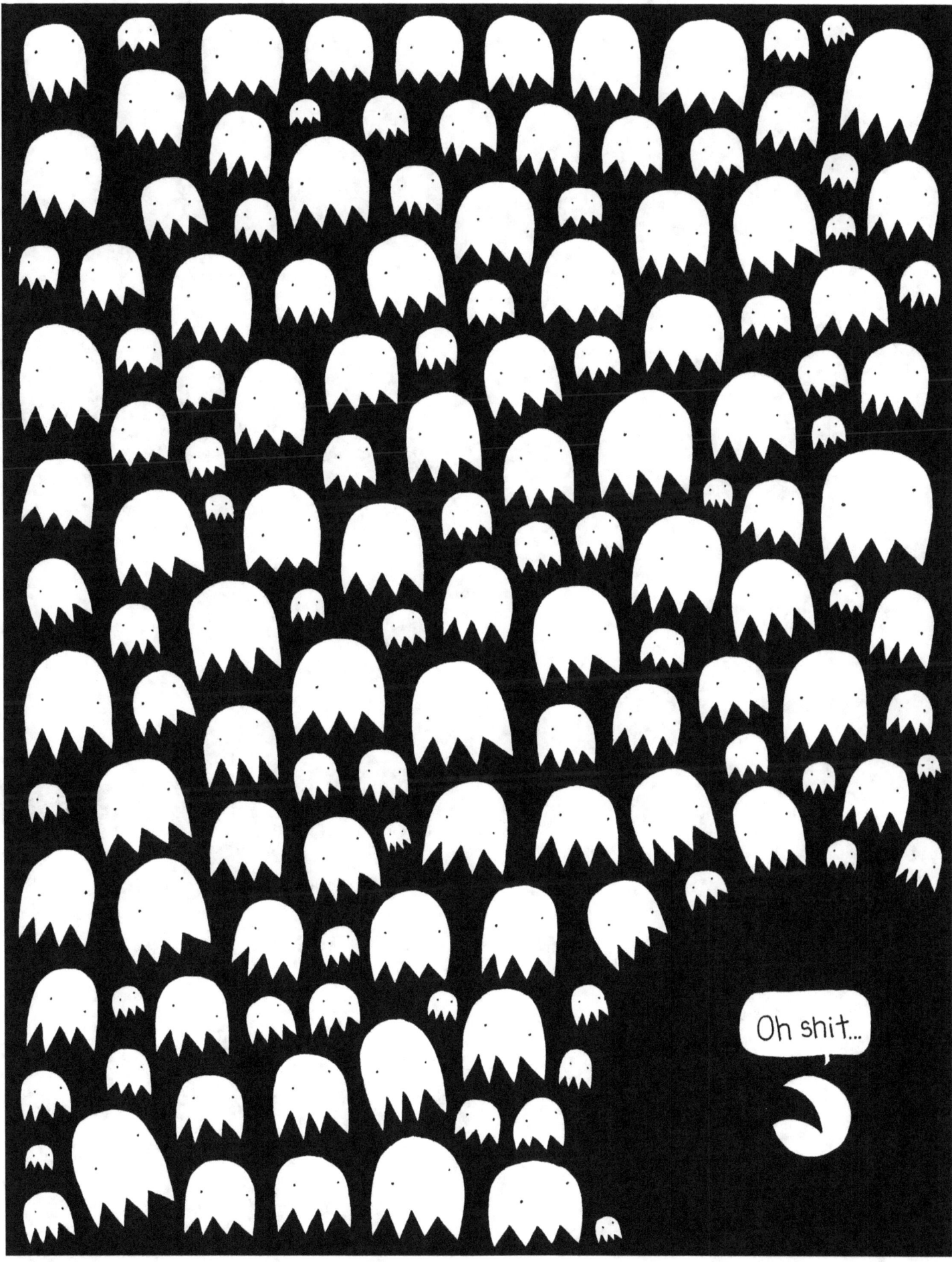

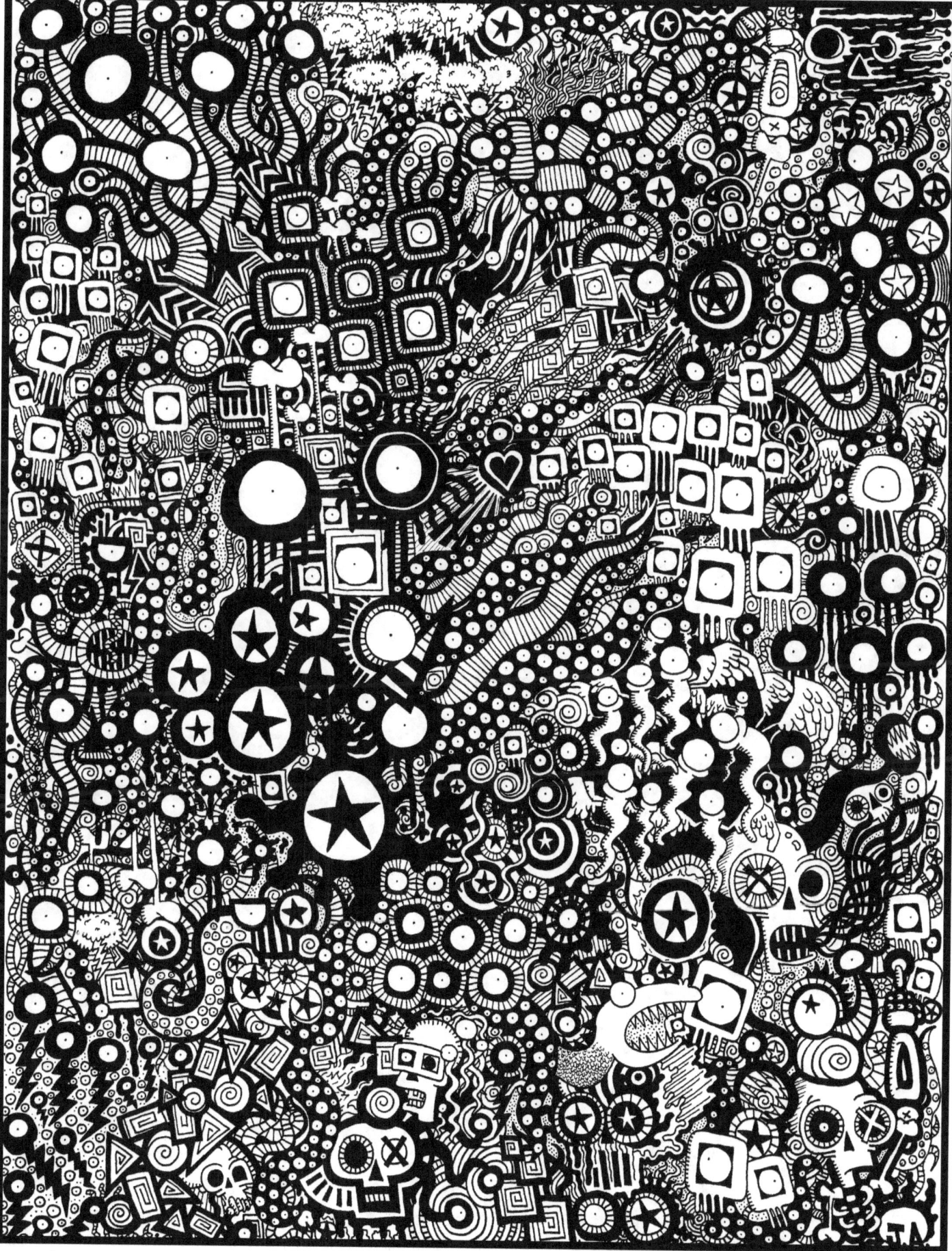

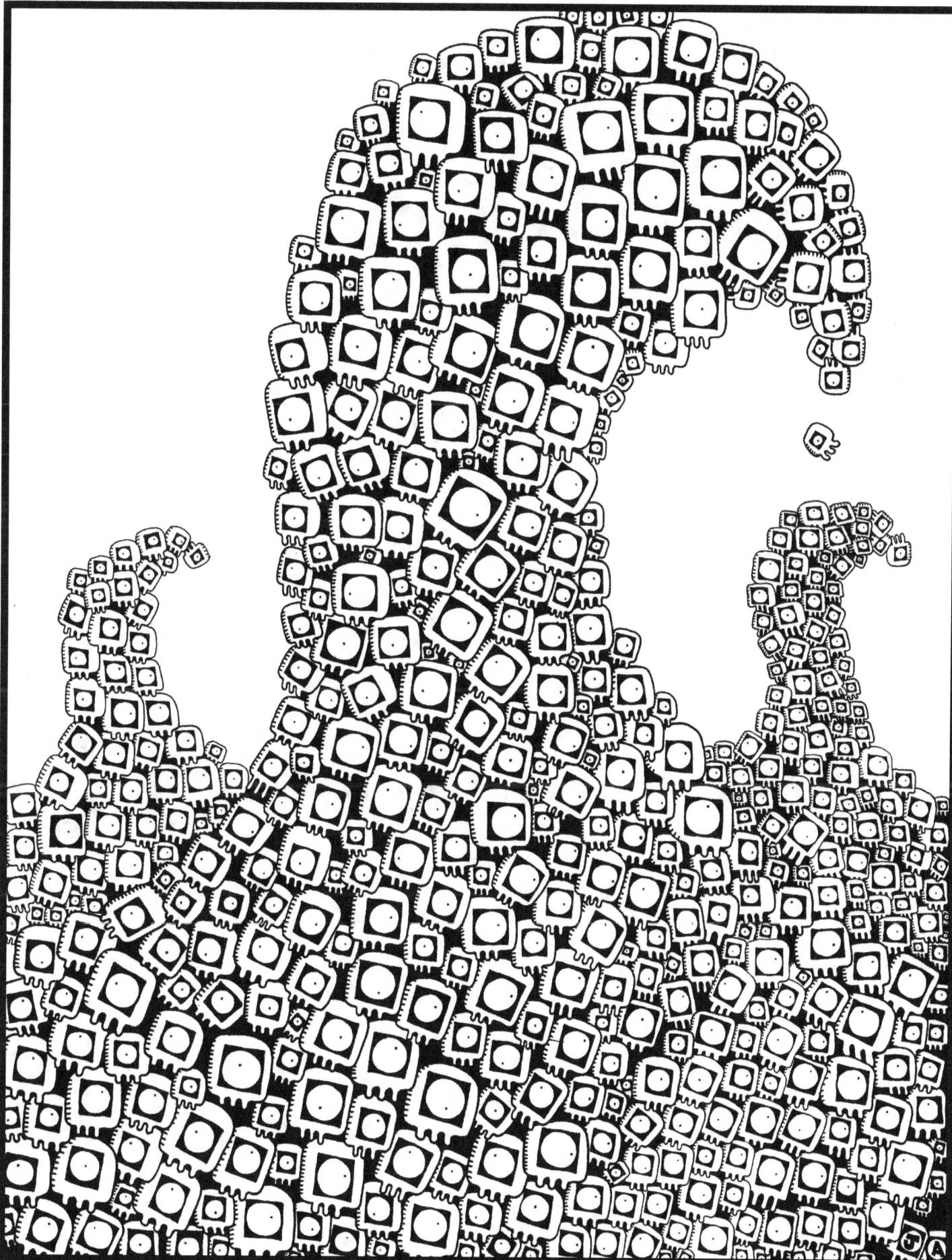

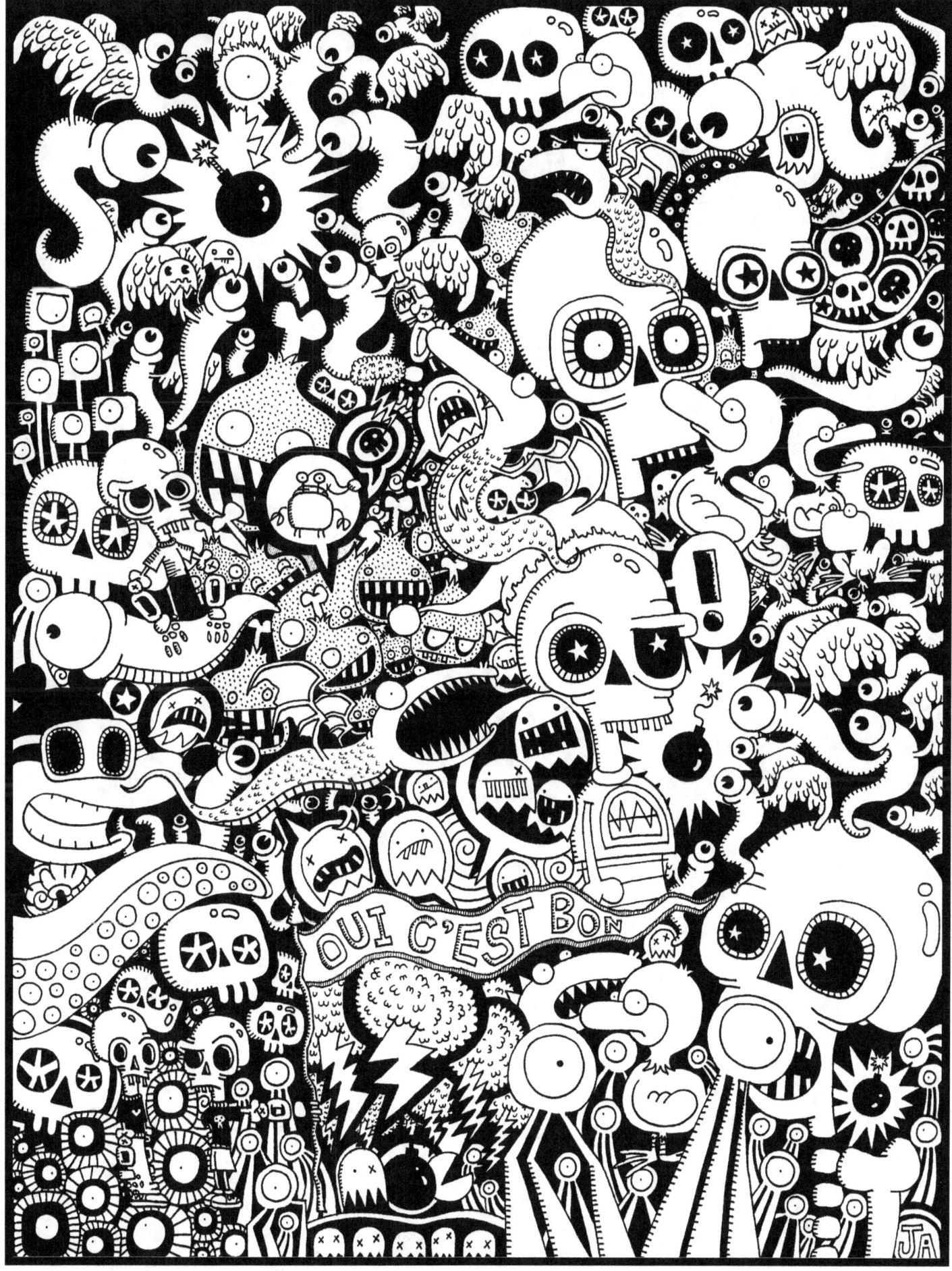

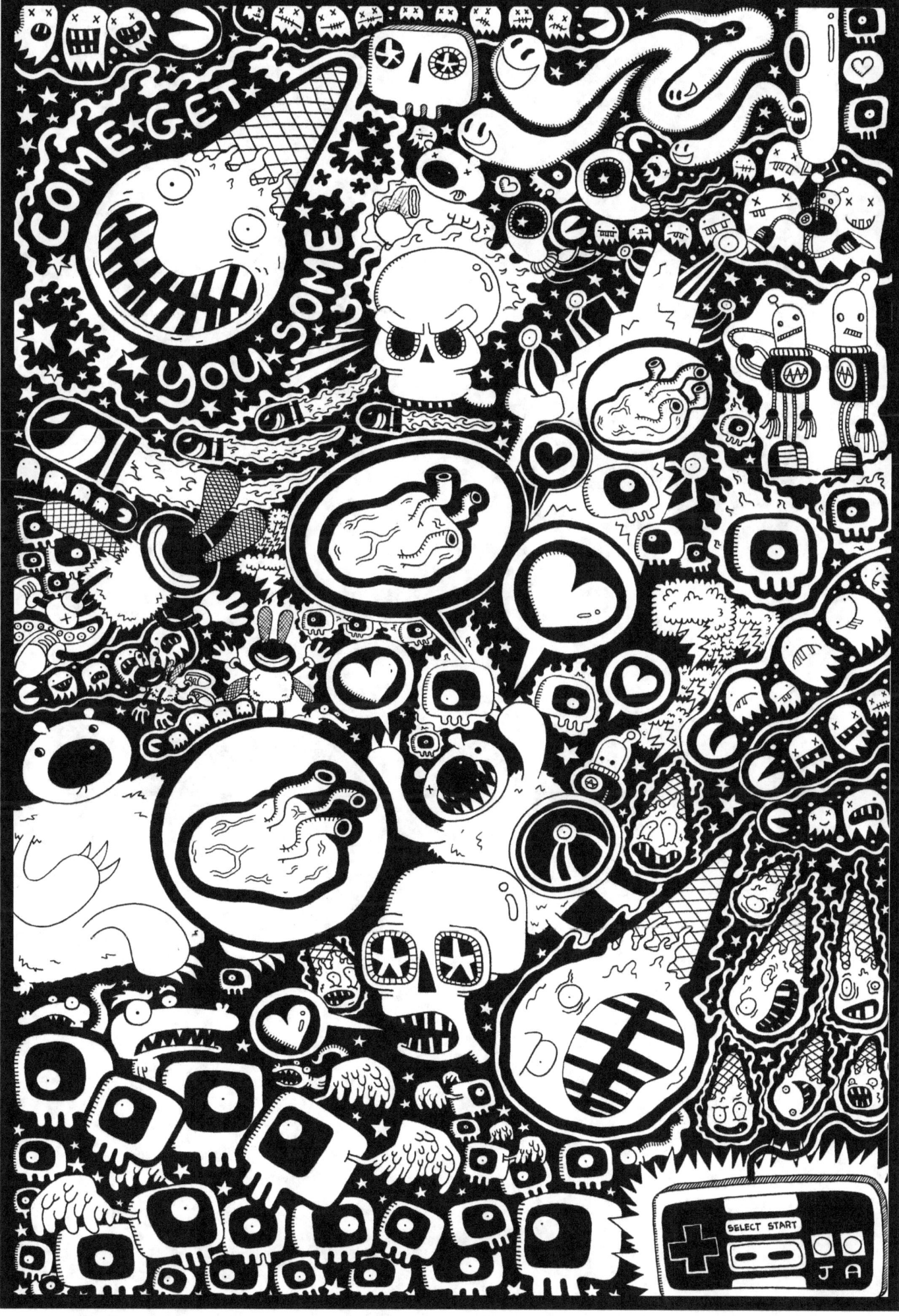

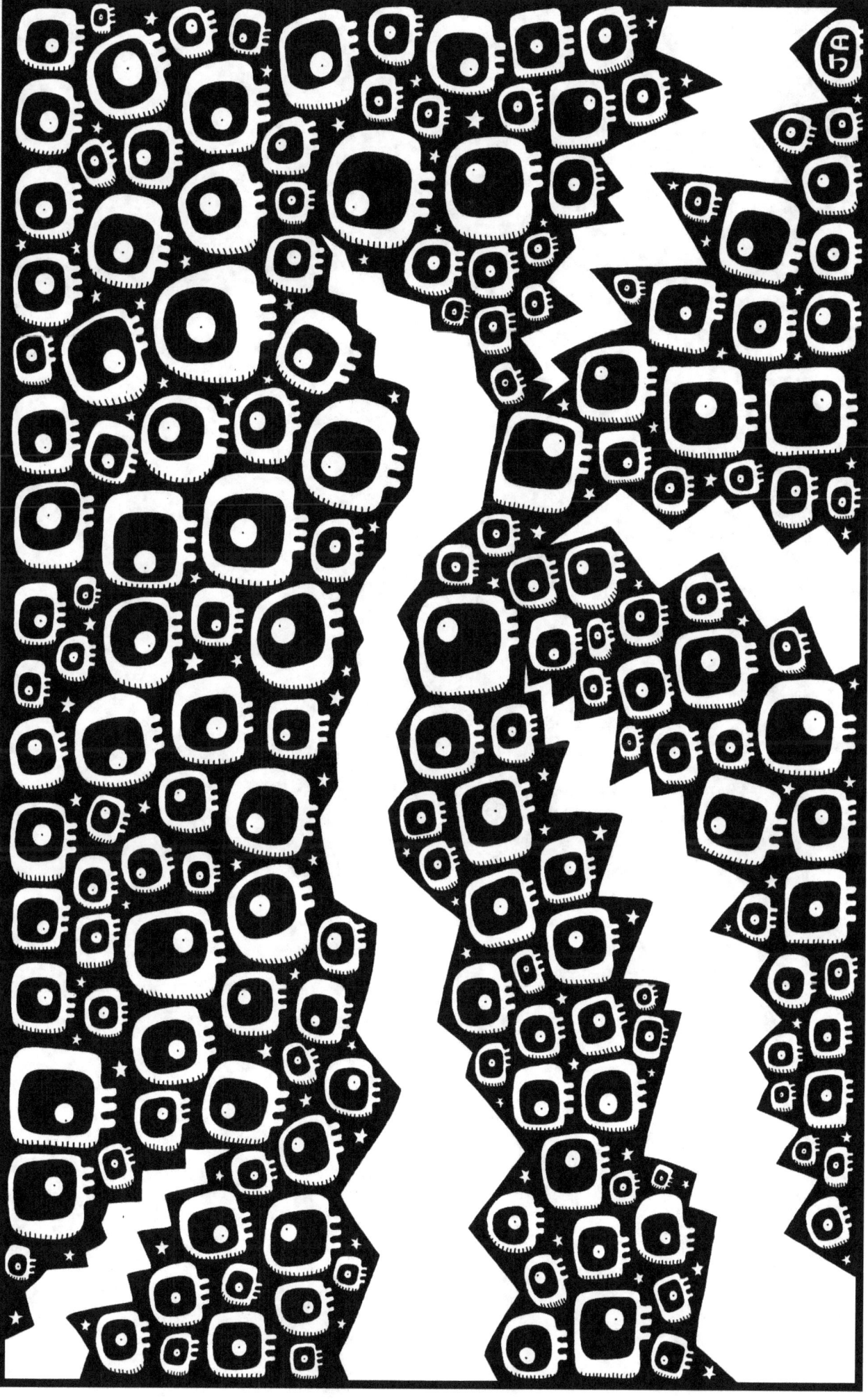

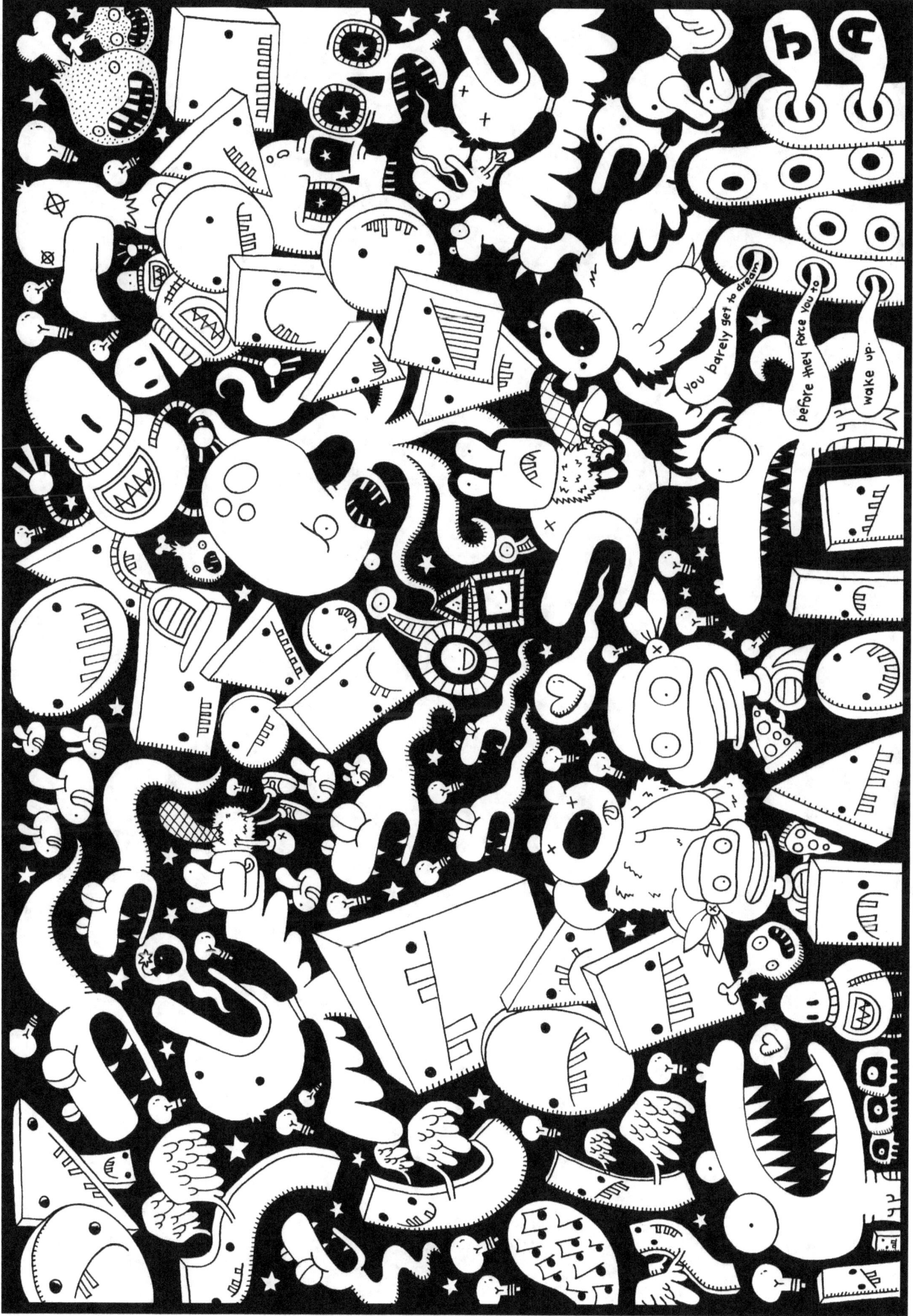

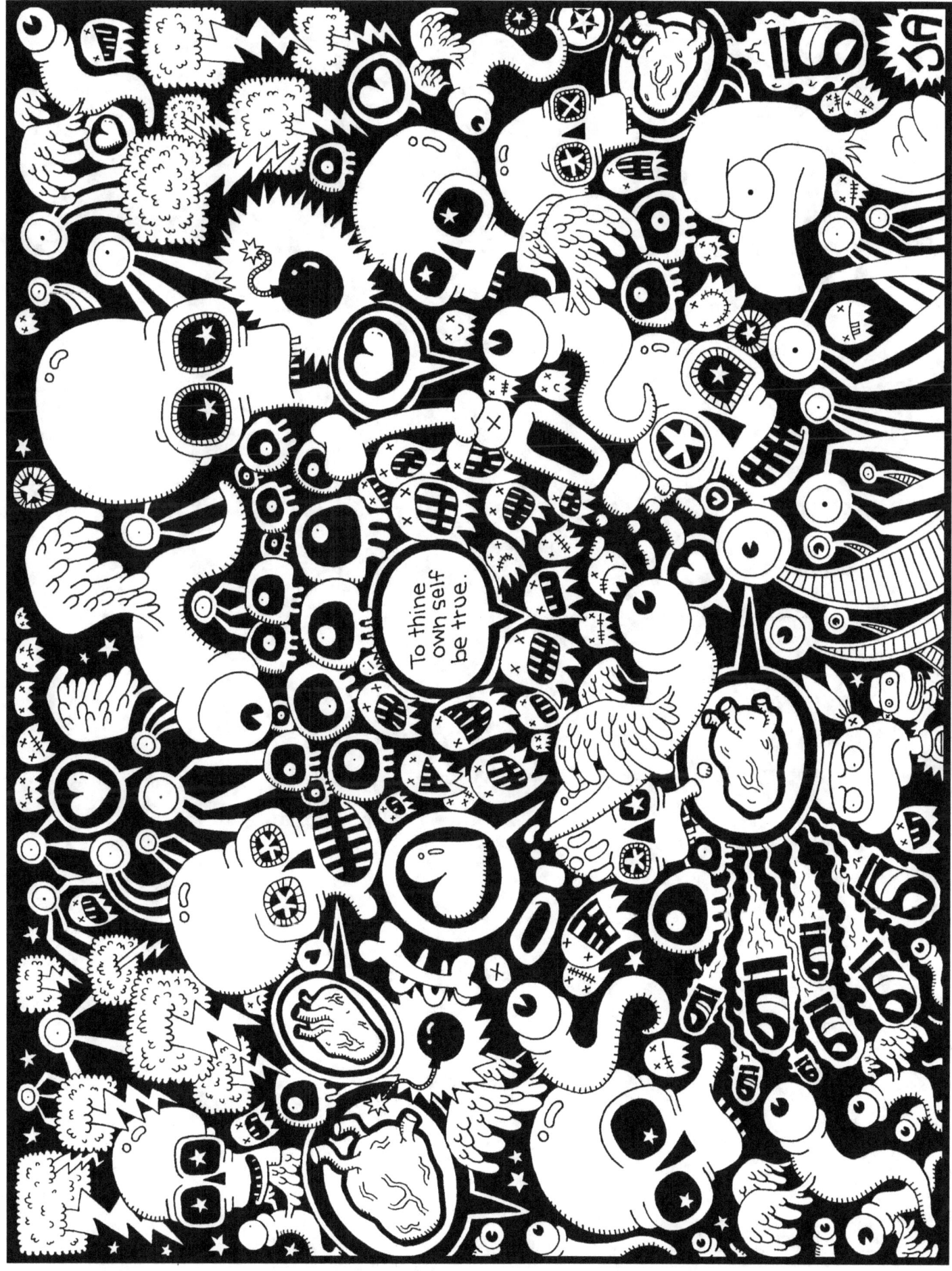

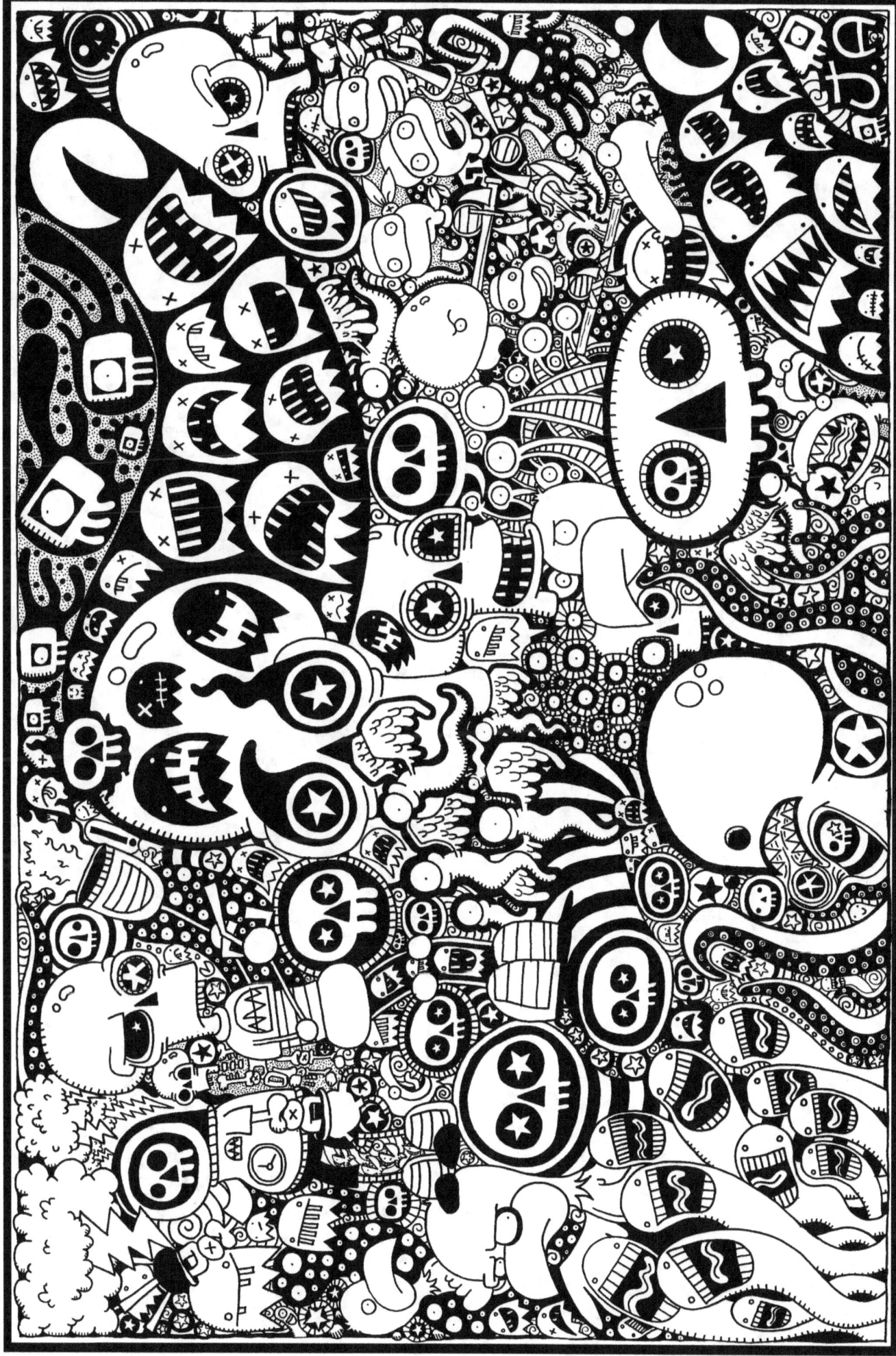

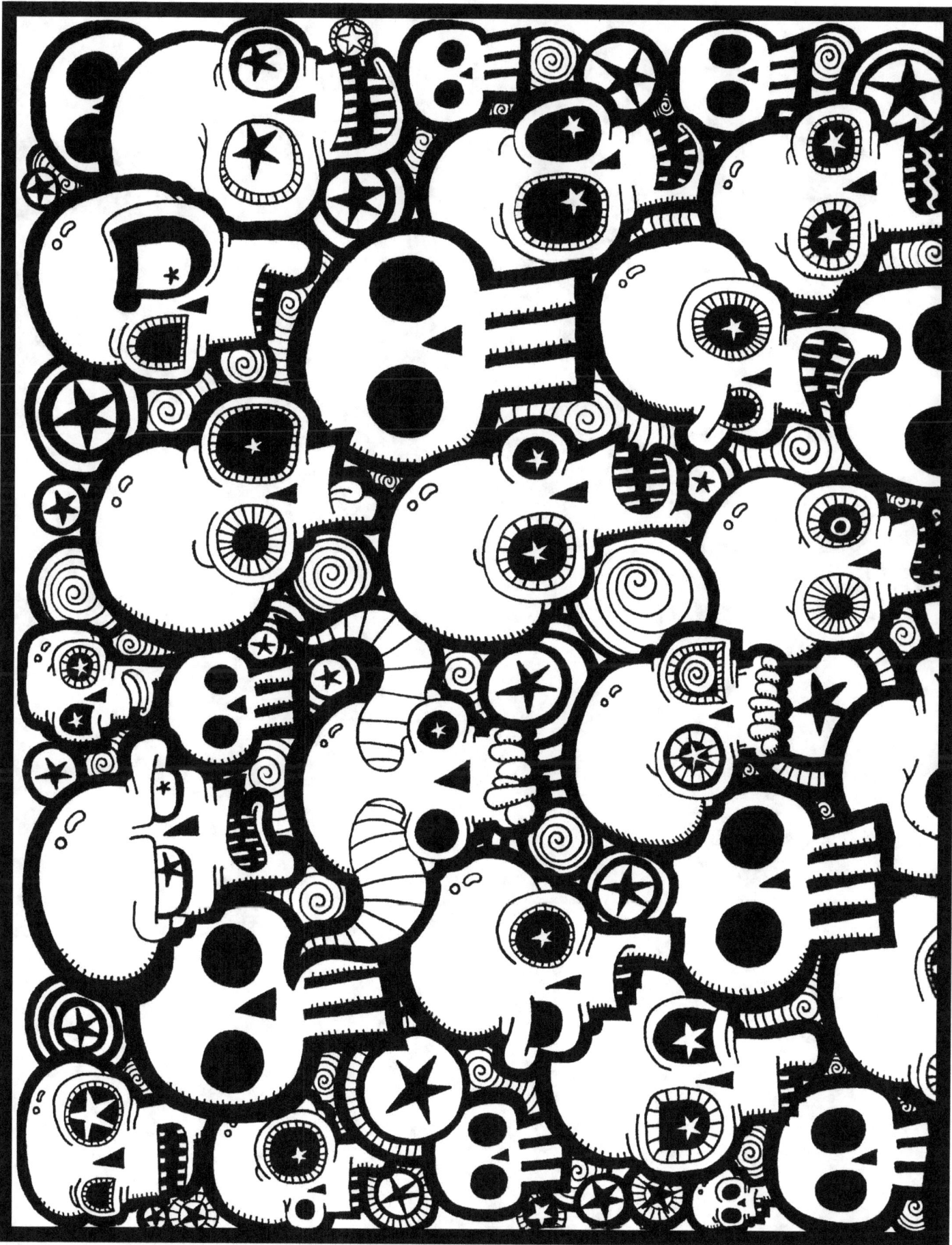

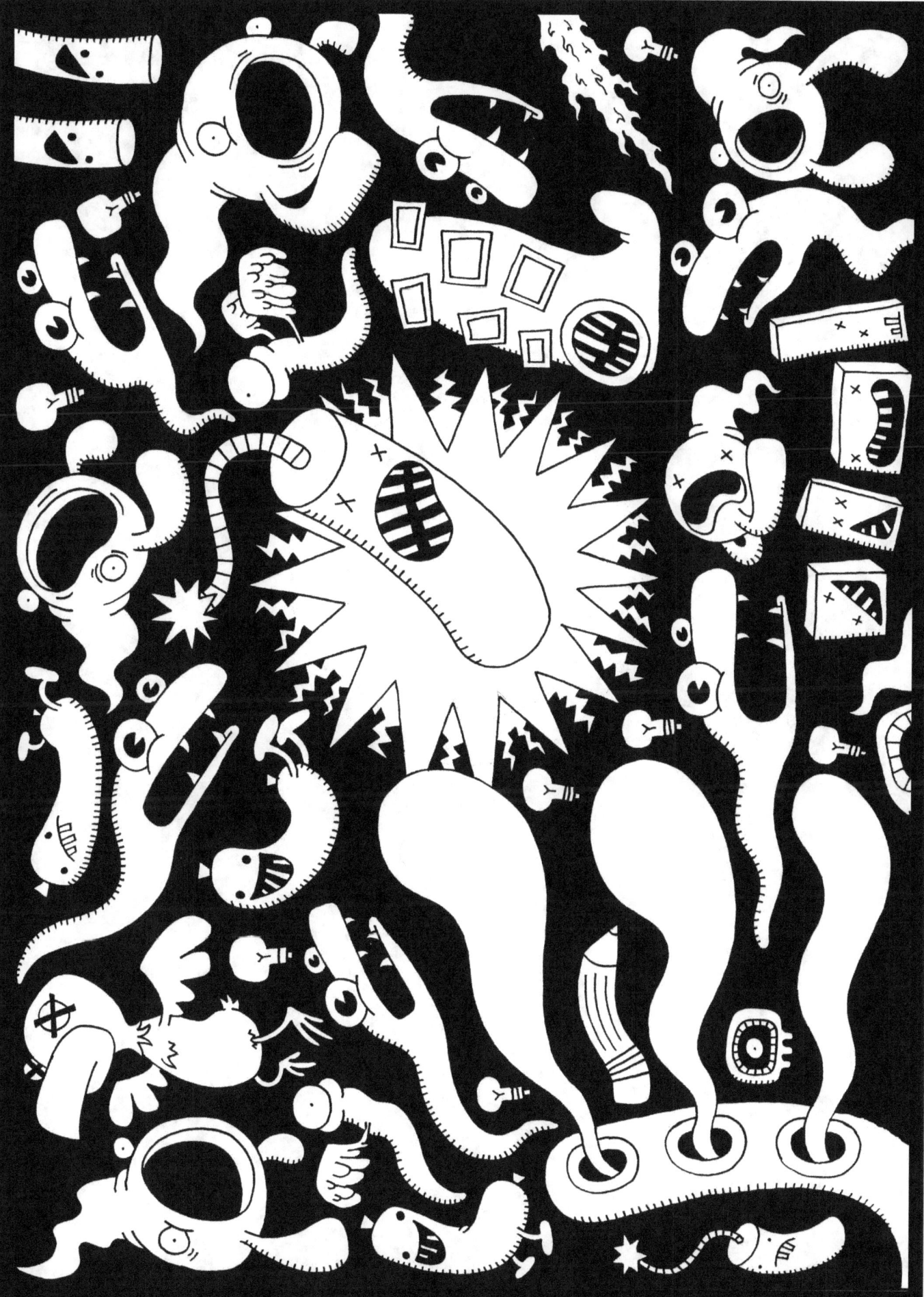

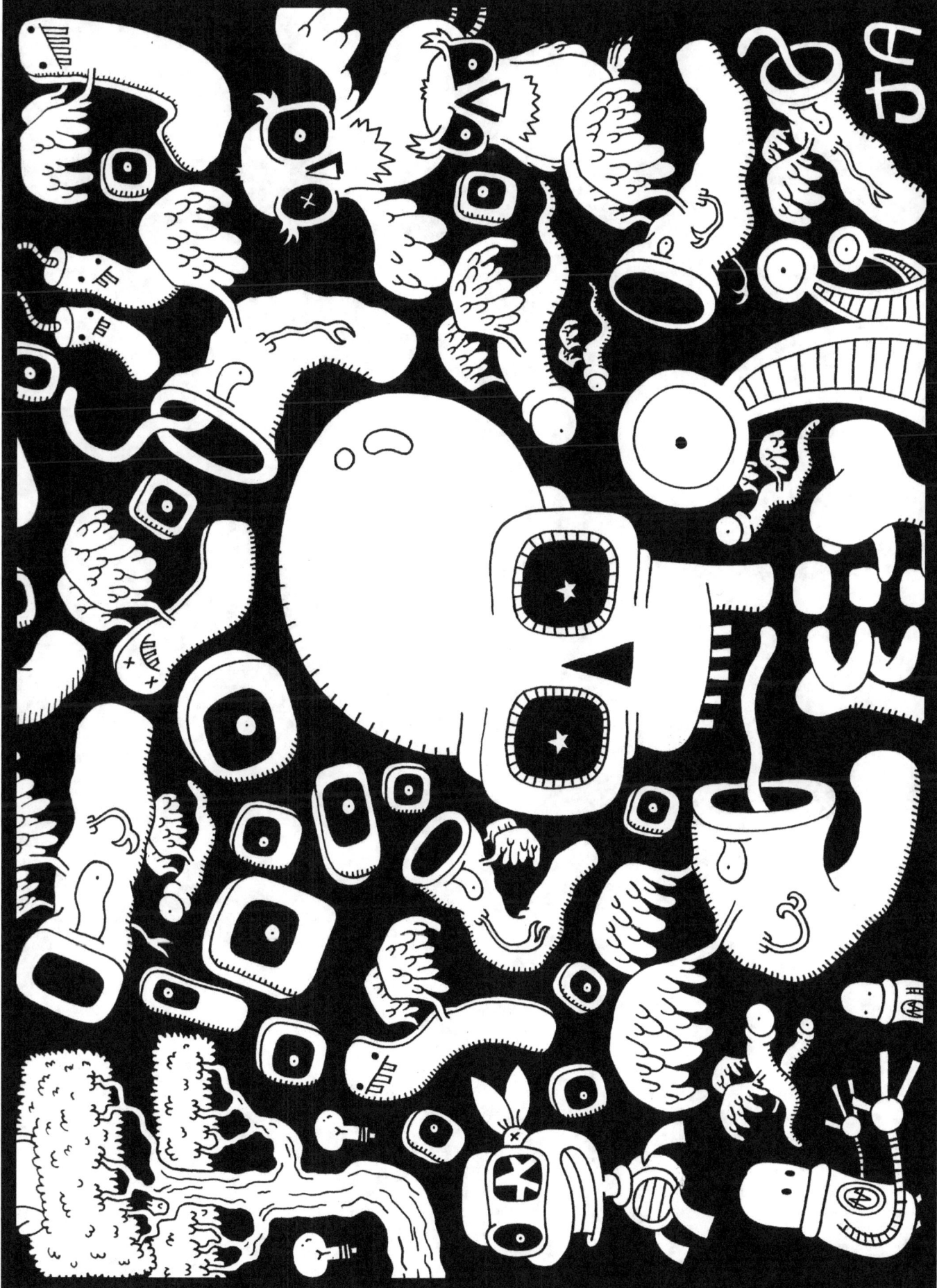

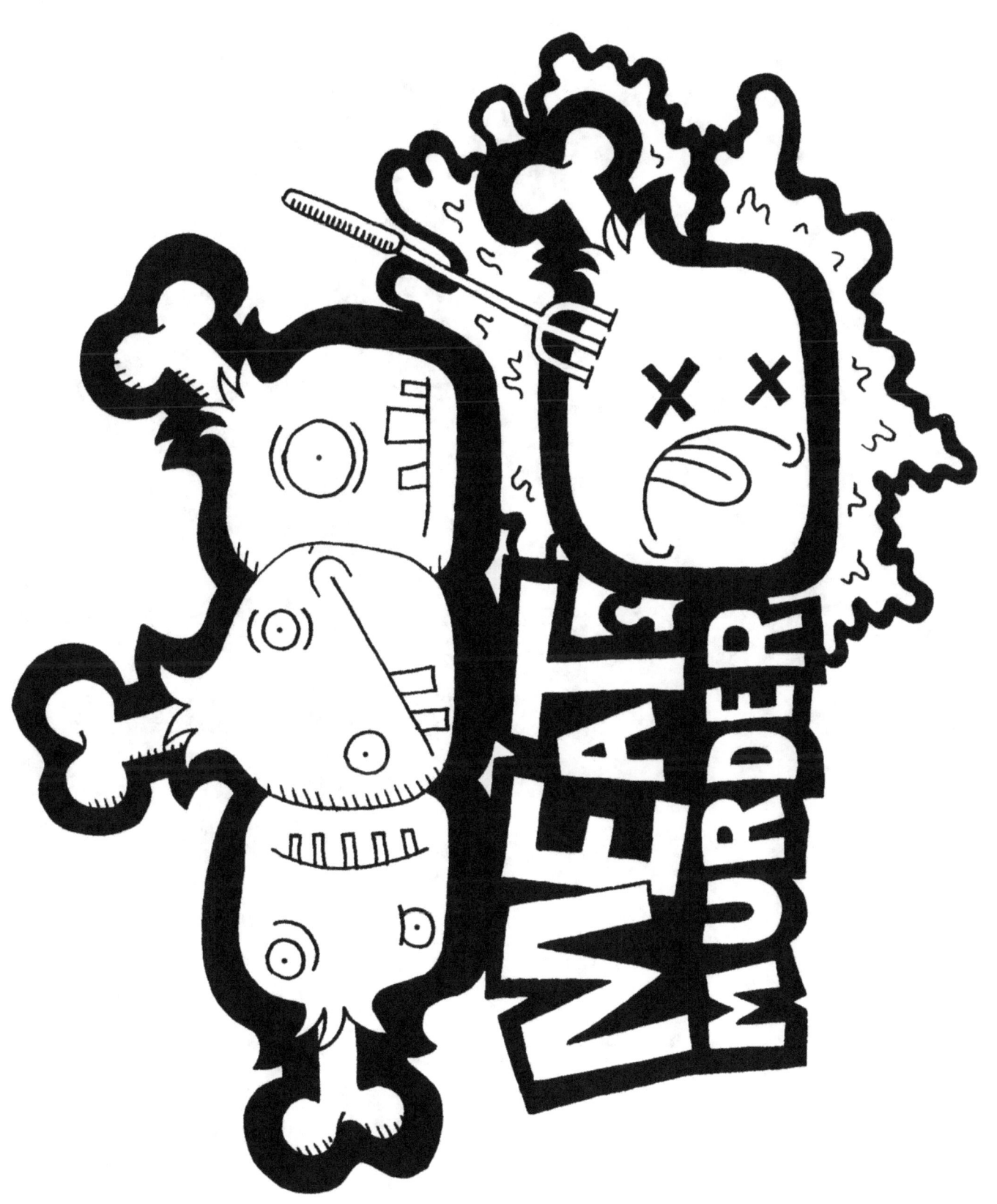

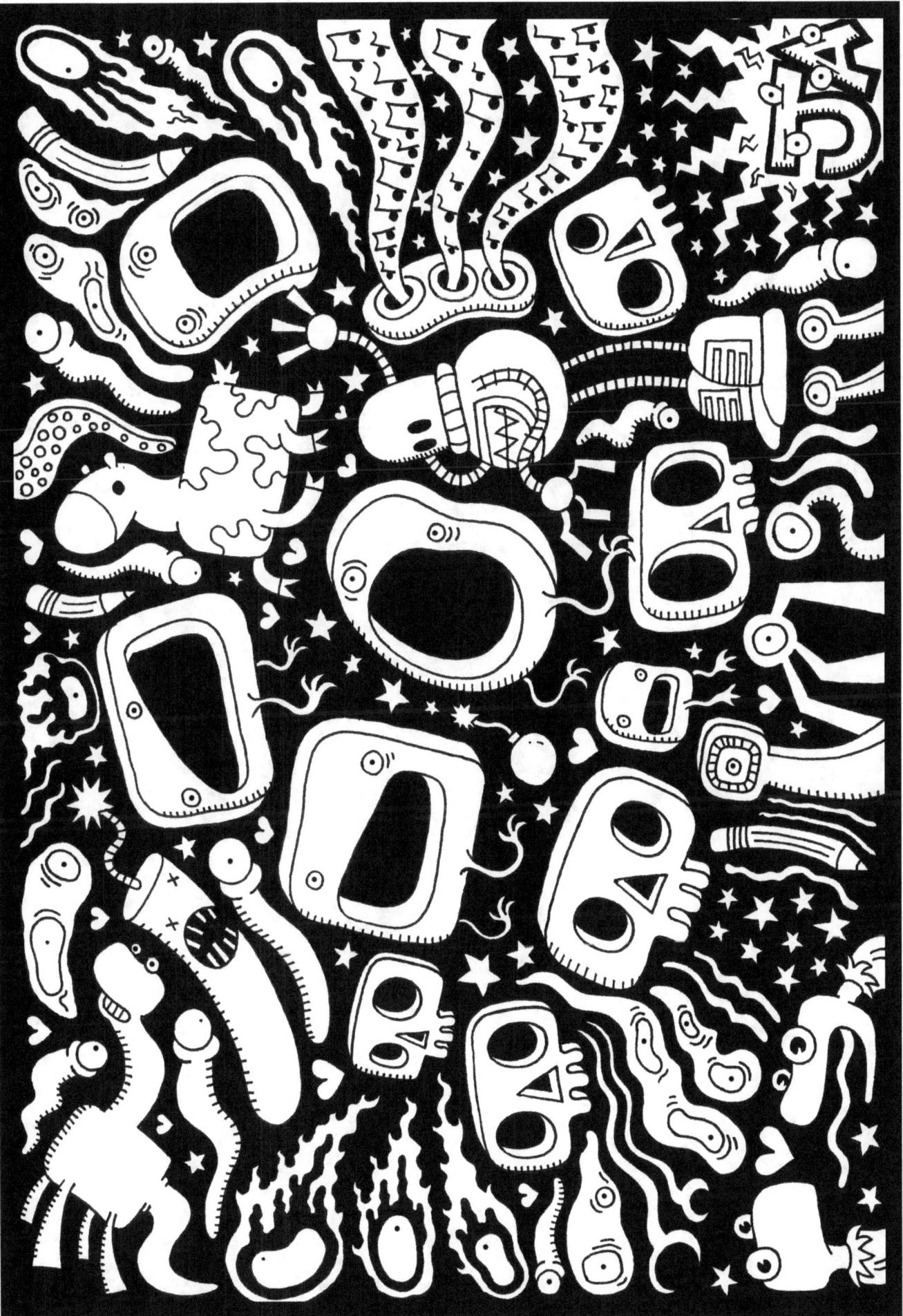

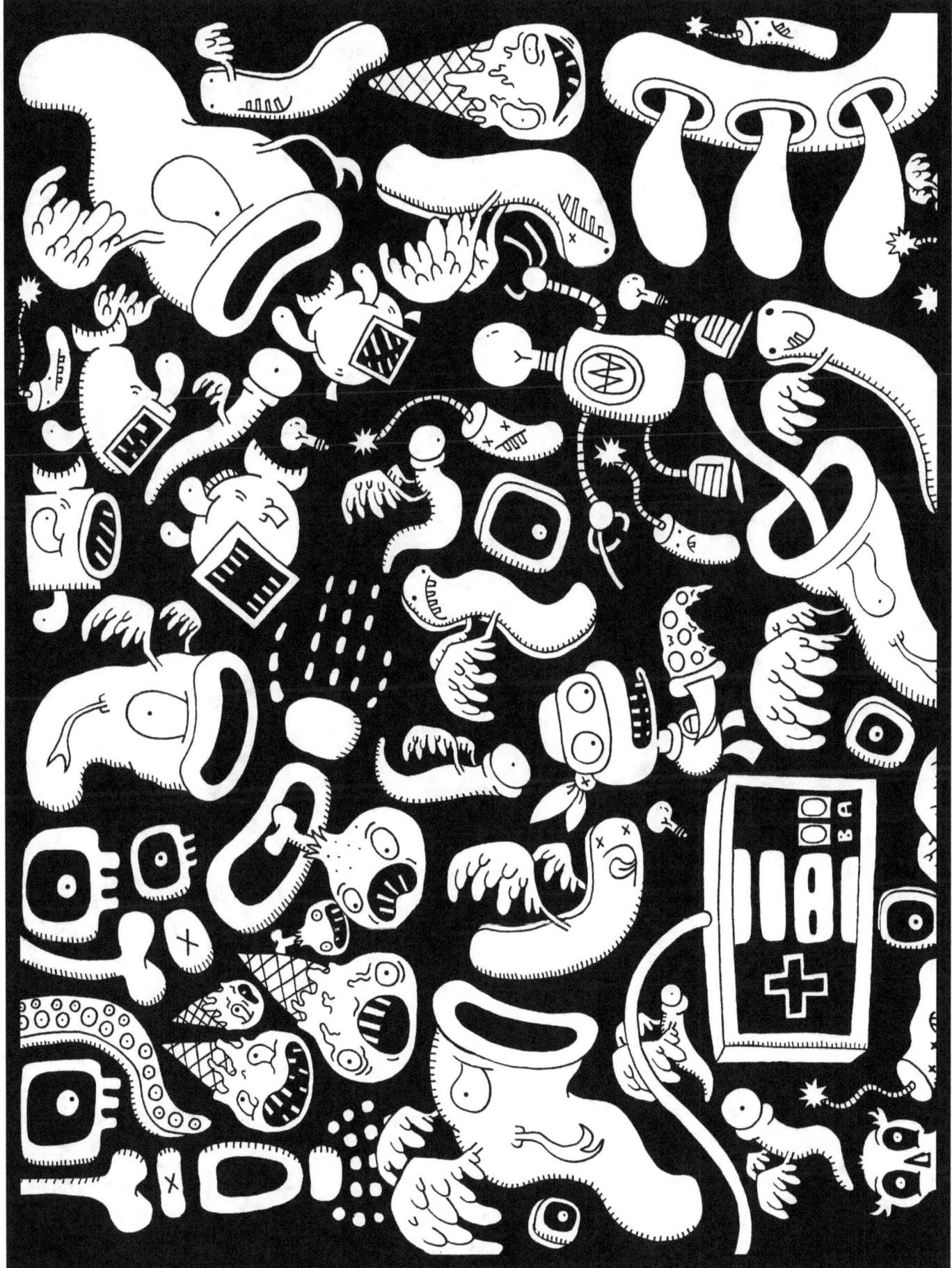

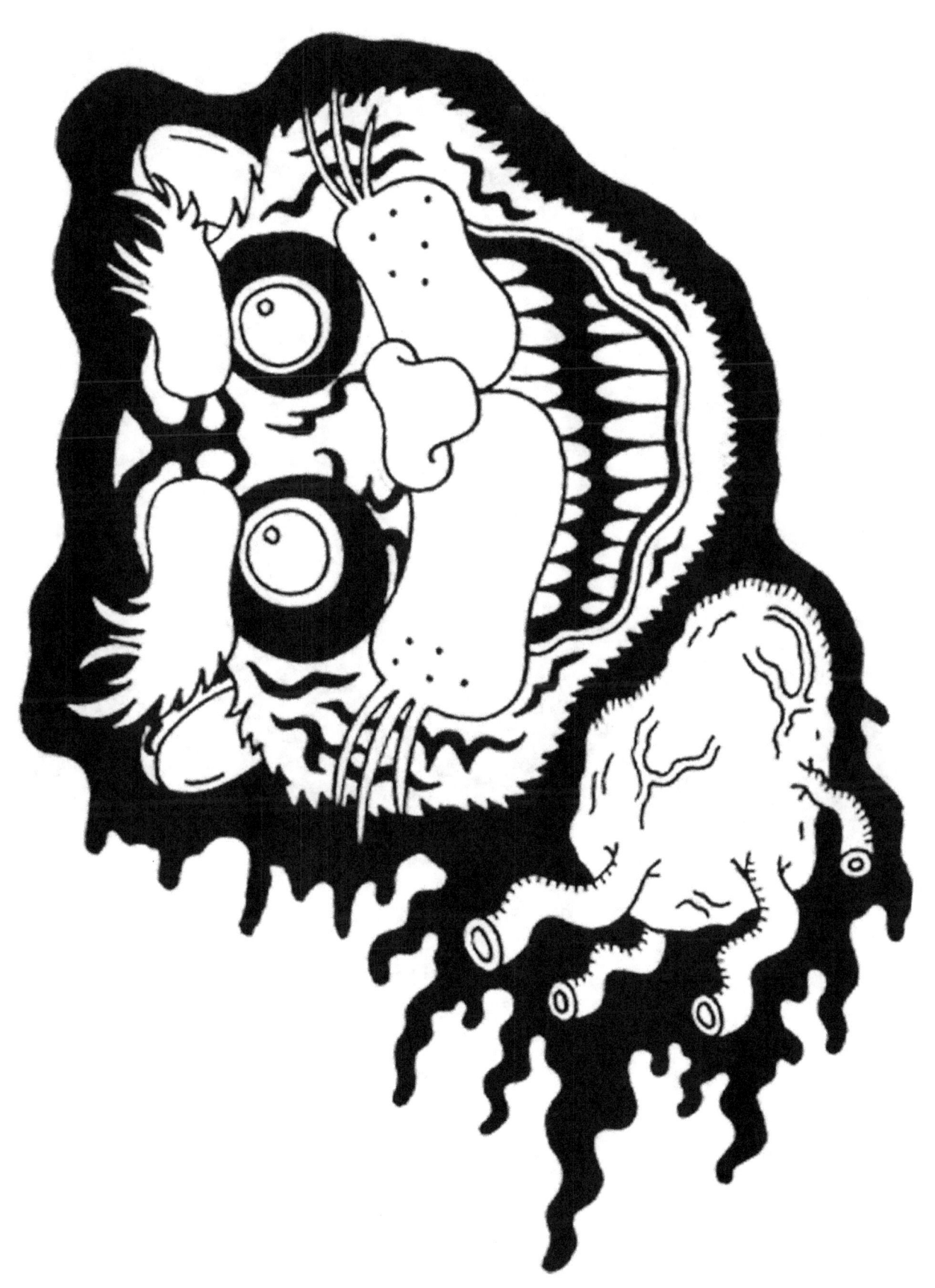

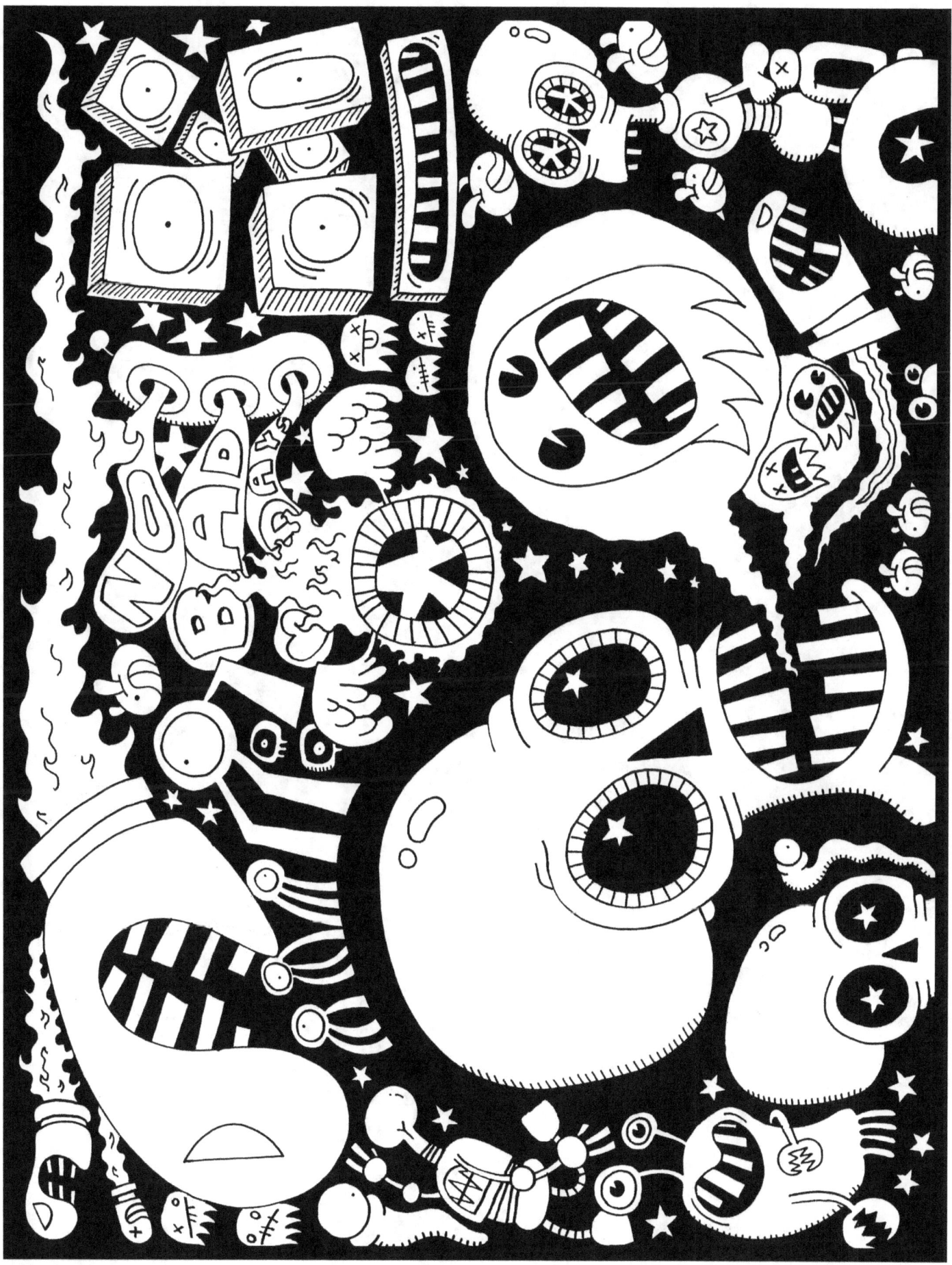

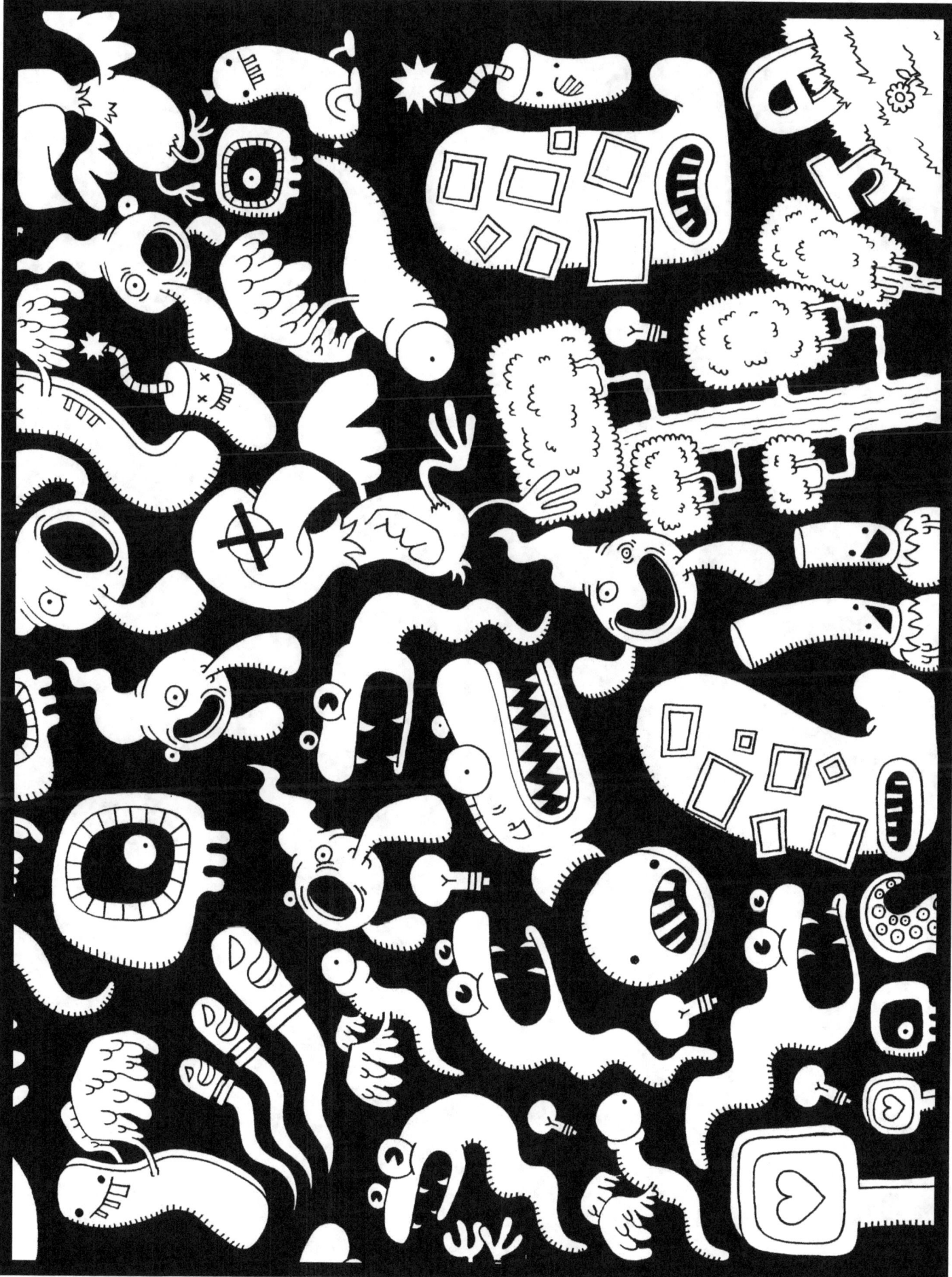

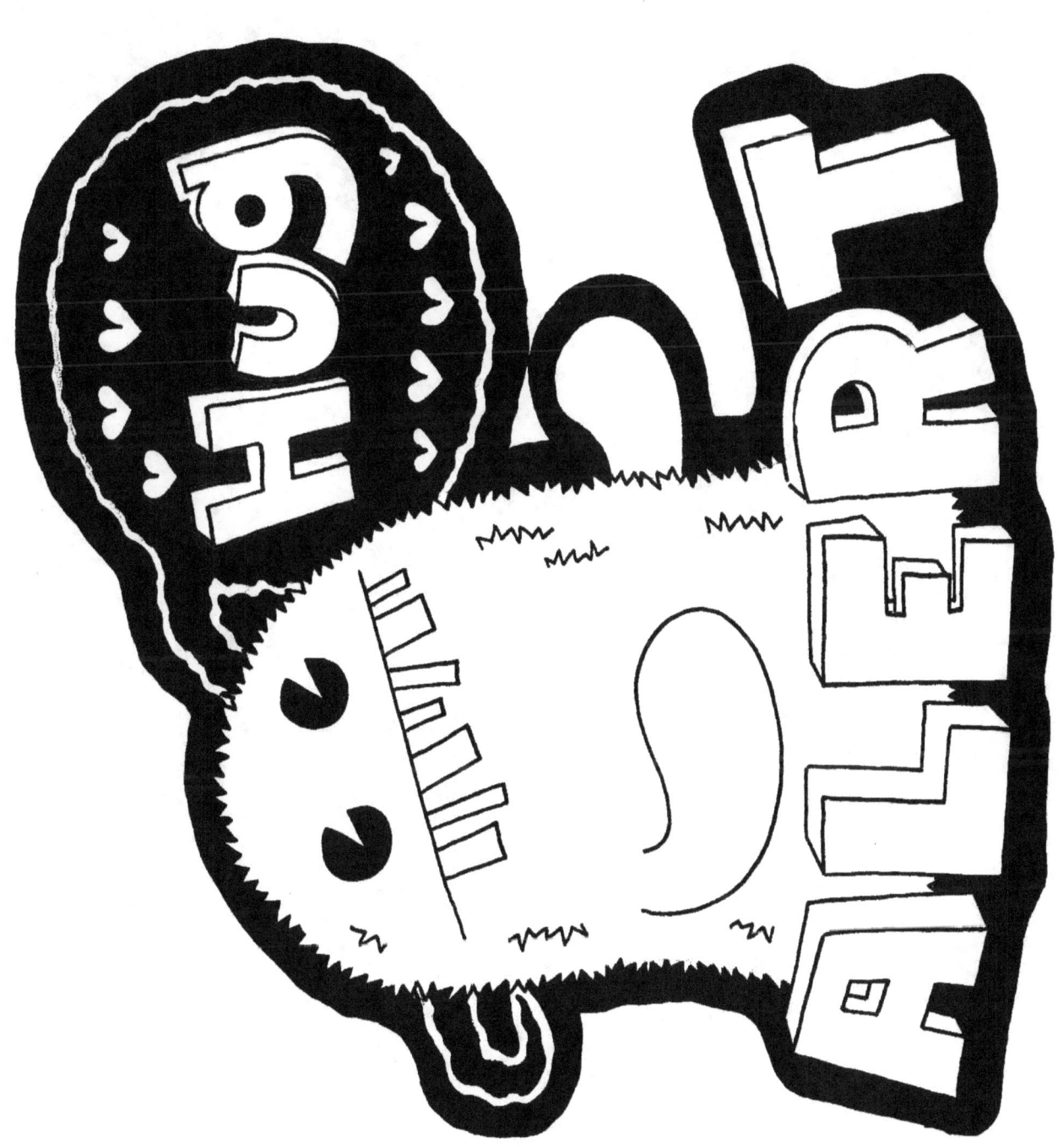

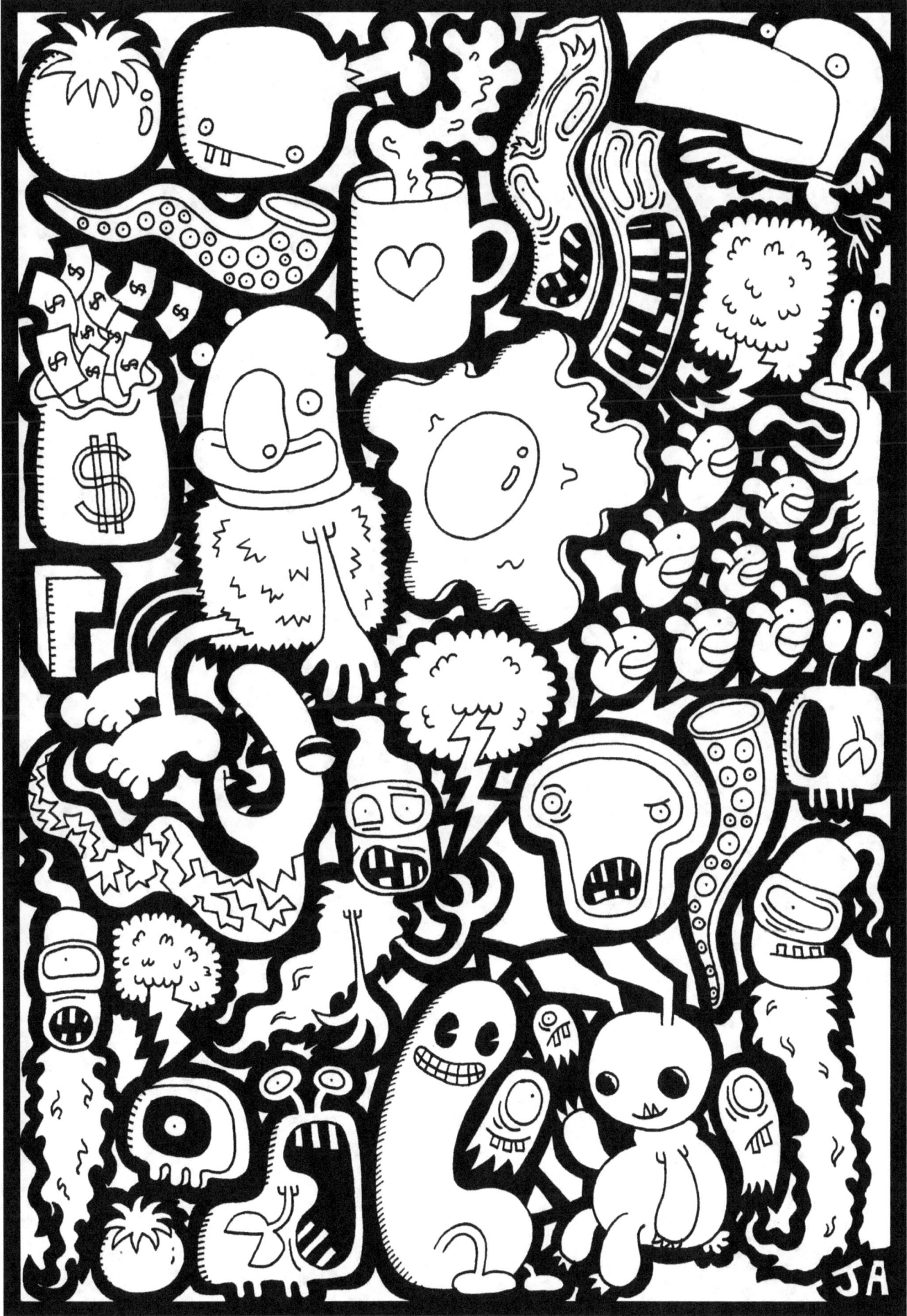

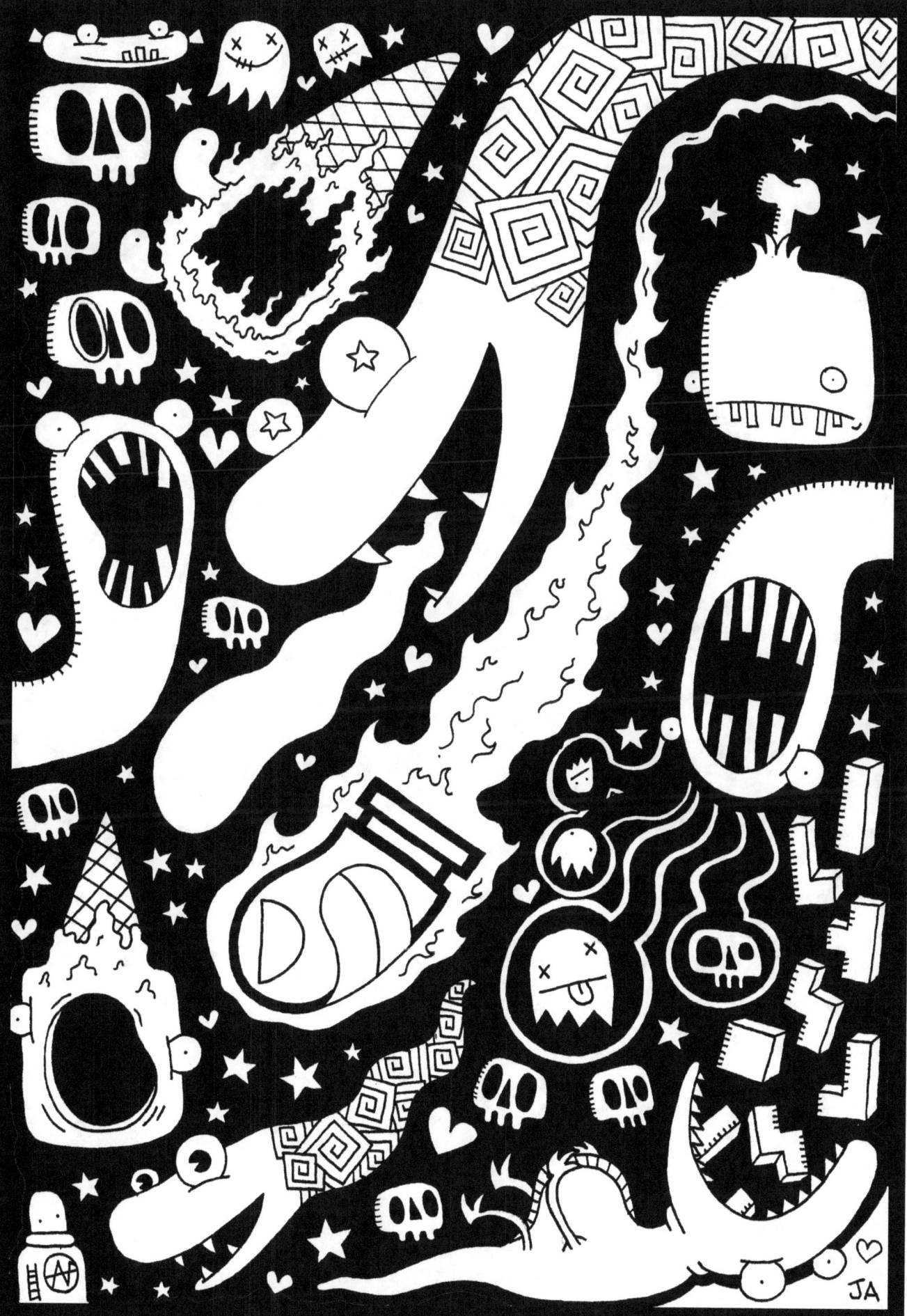

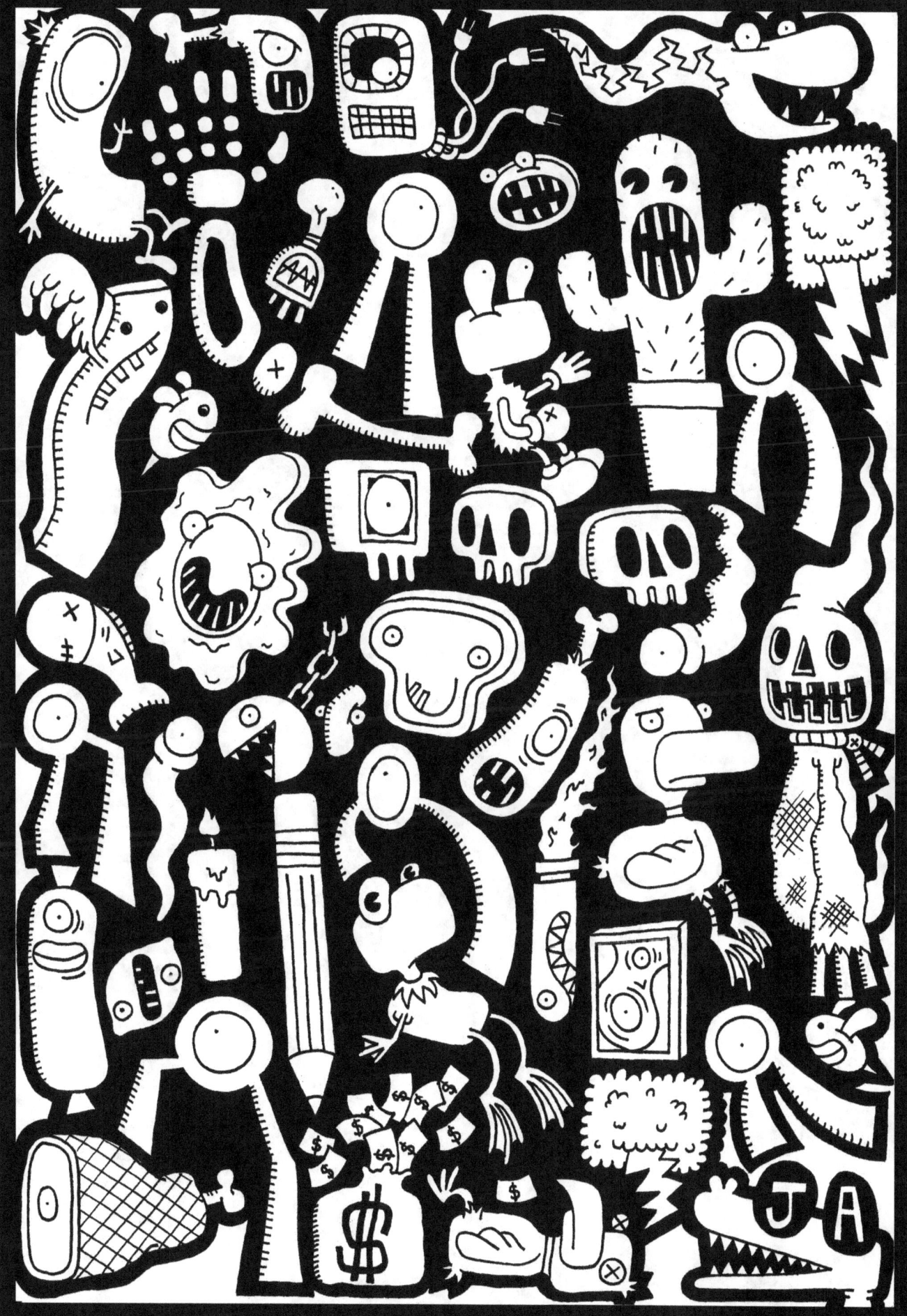

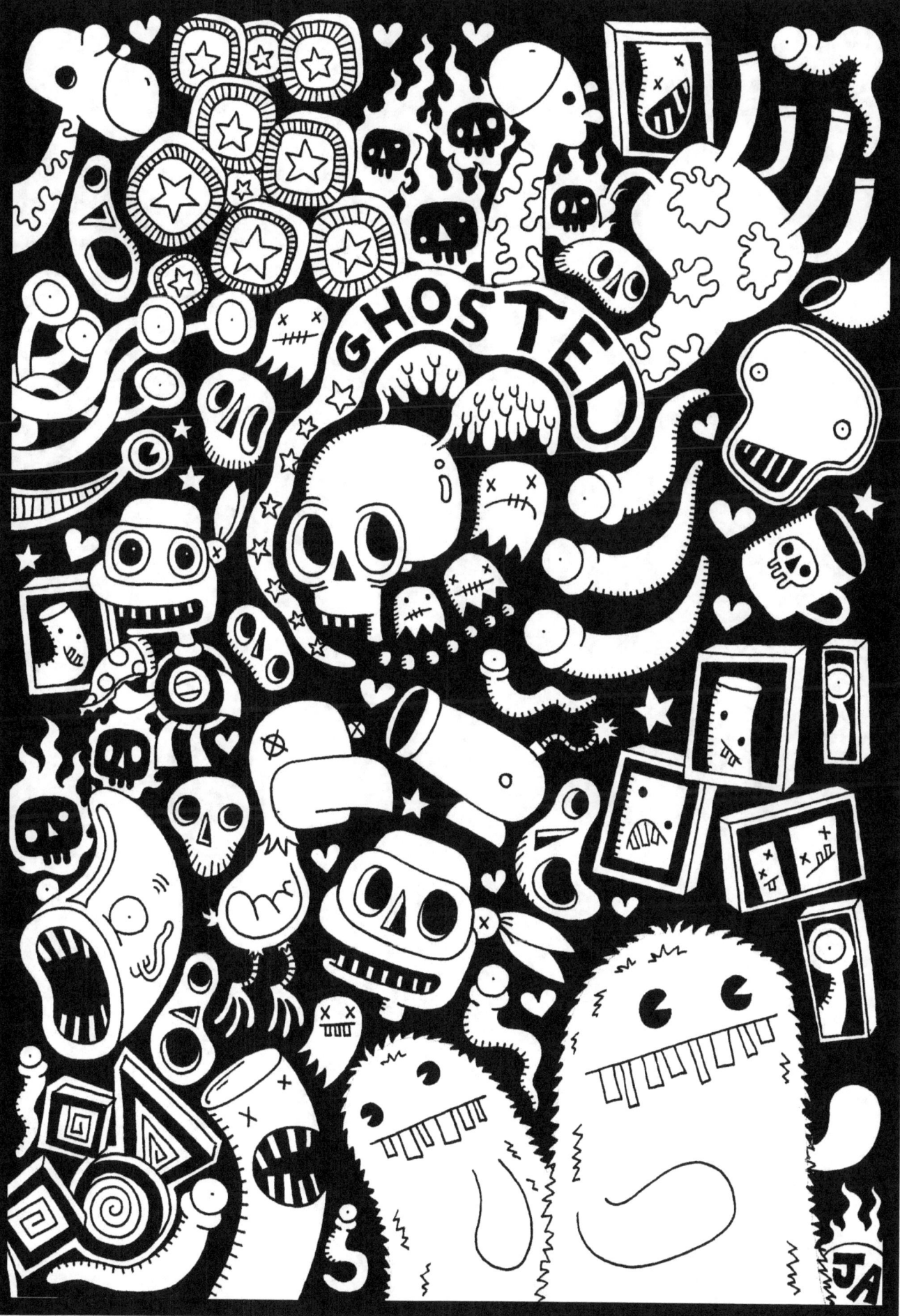

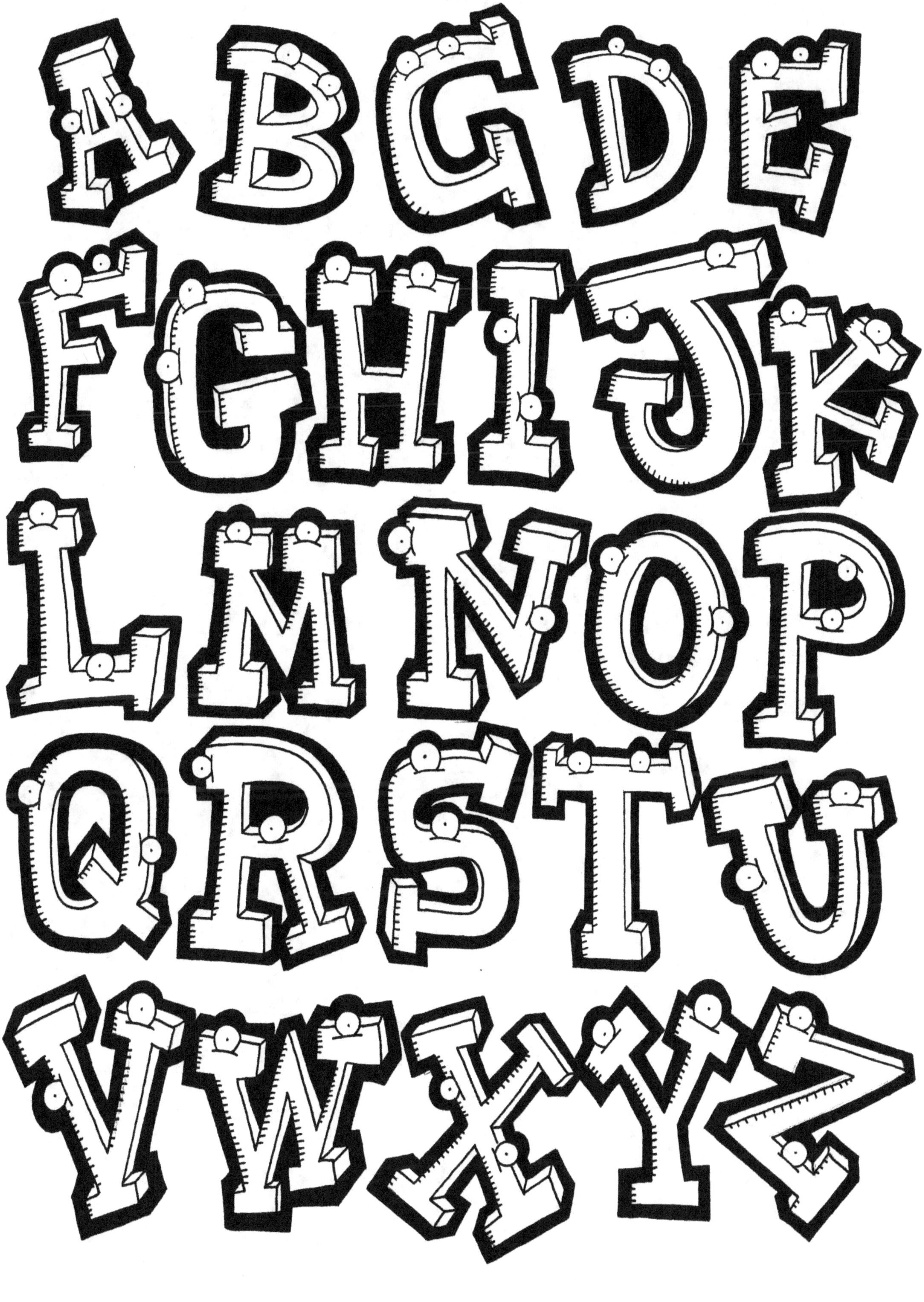
A B C D E
F G H I J K
L M N O P
Q R S T U
V W X Y Z

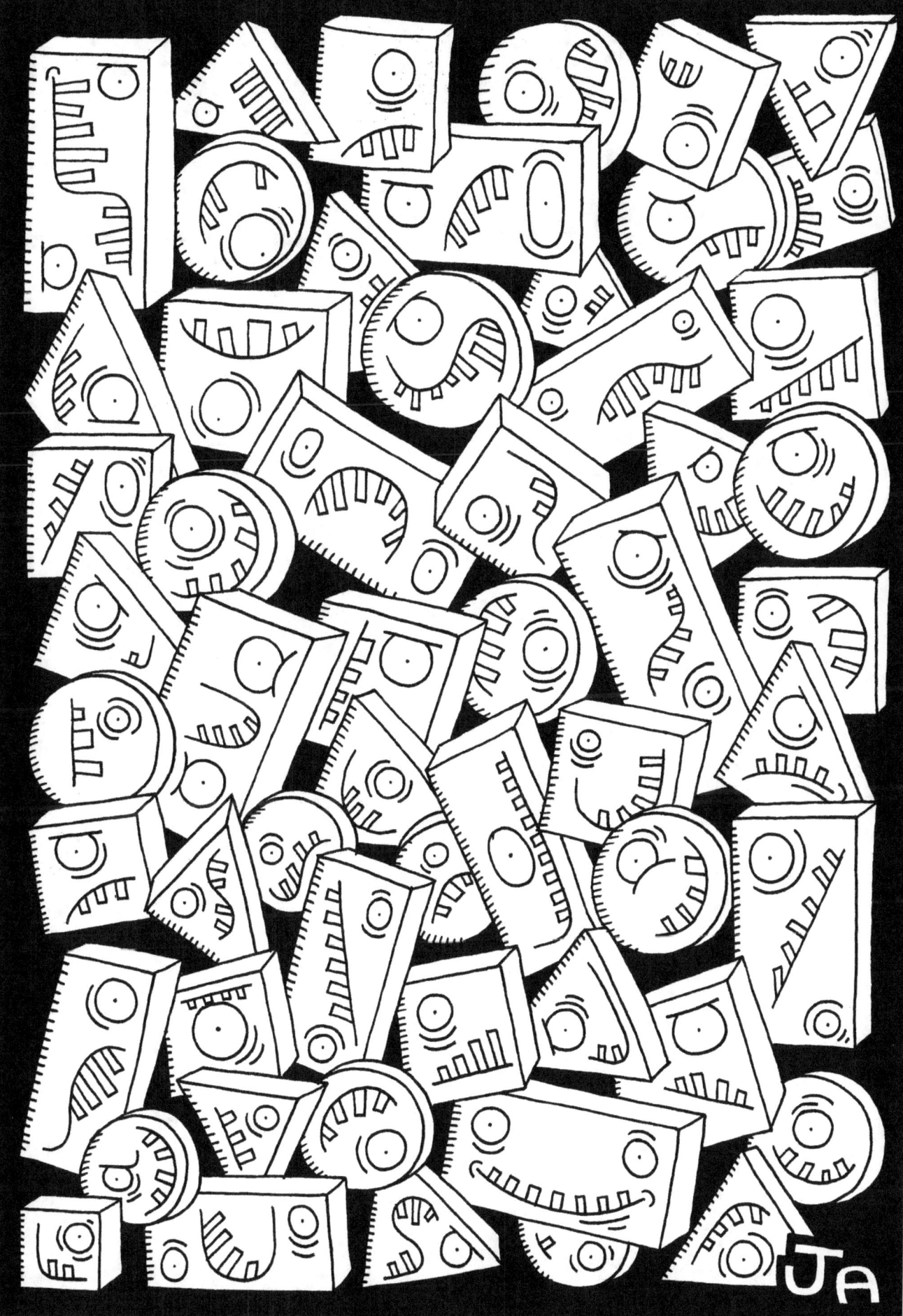

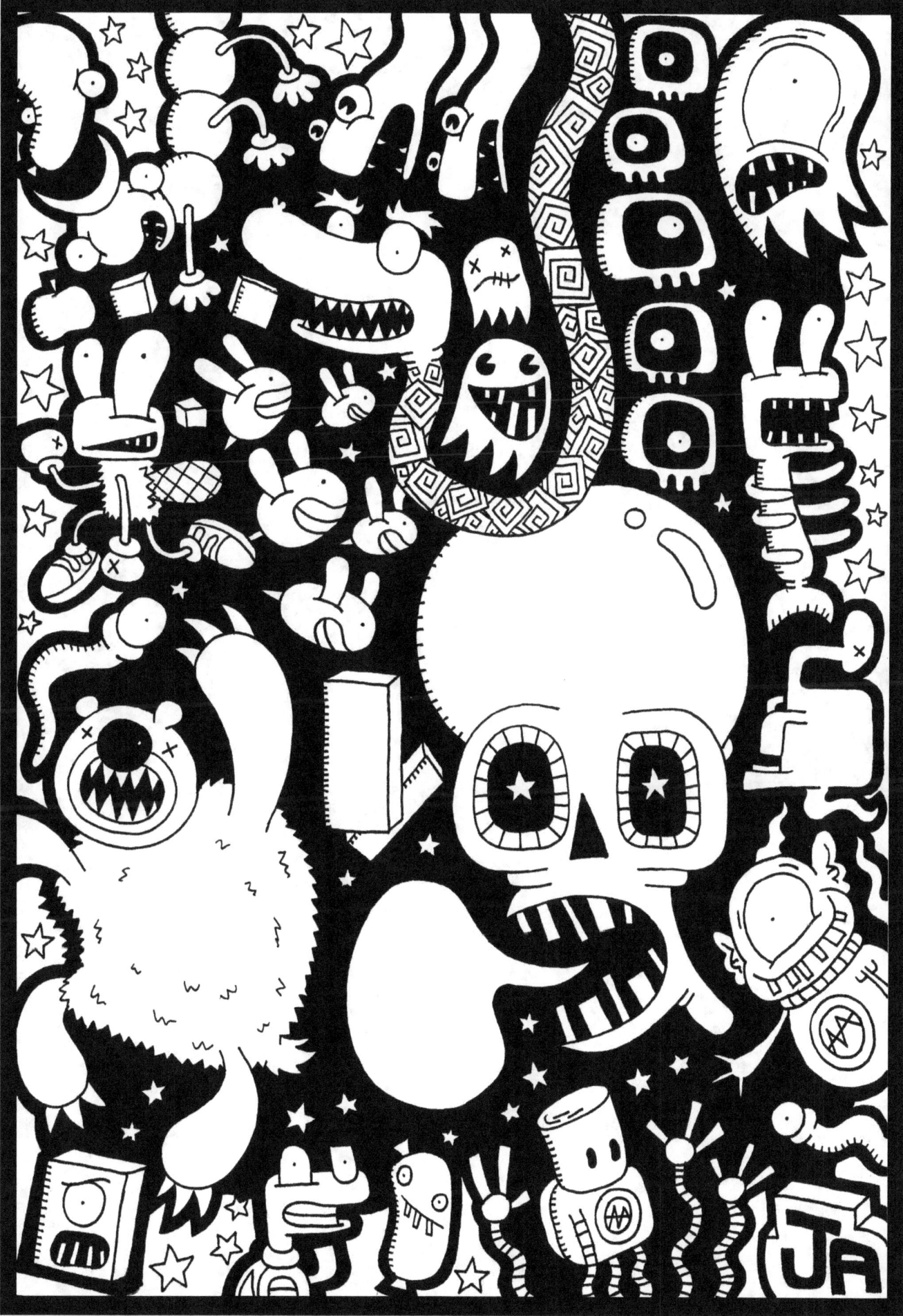

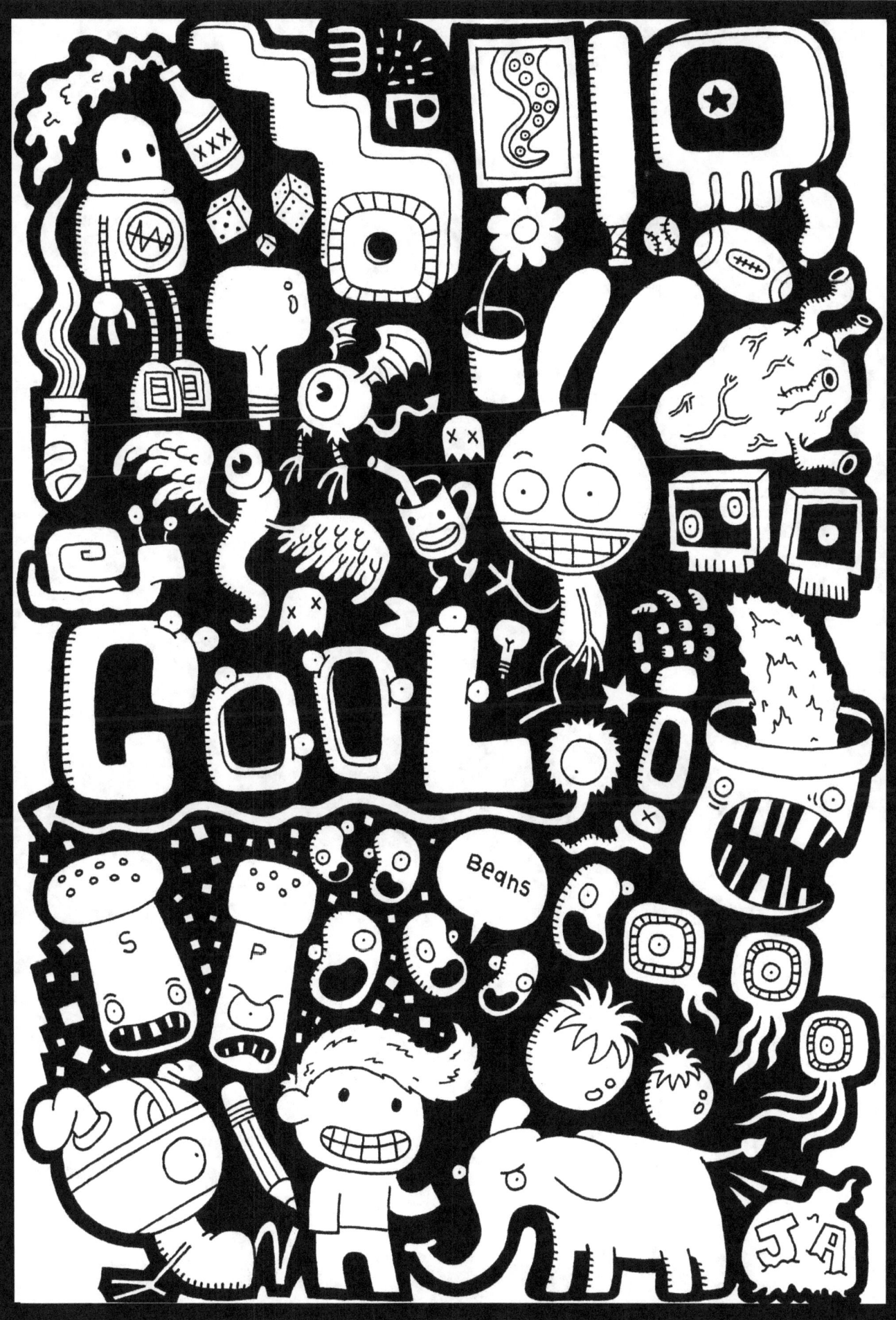

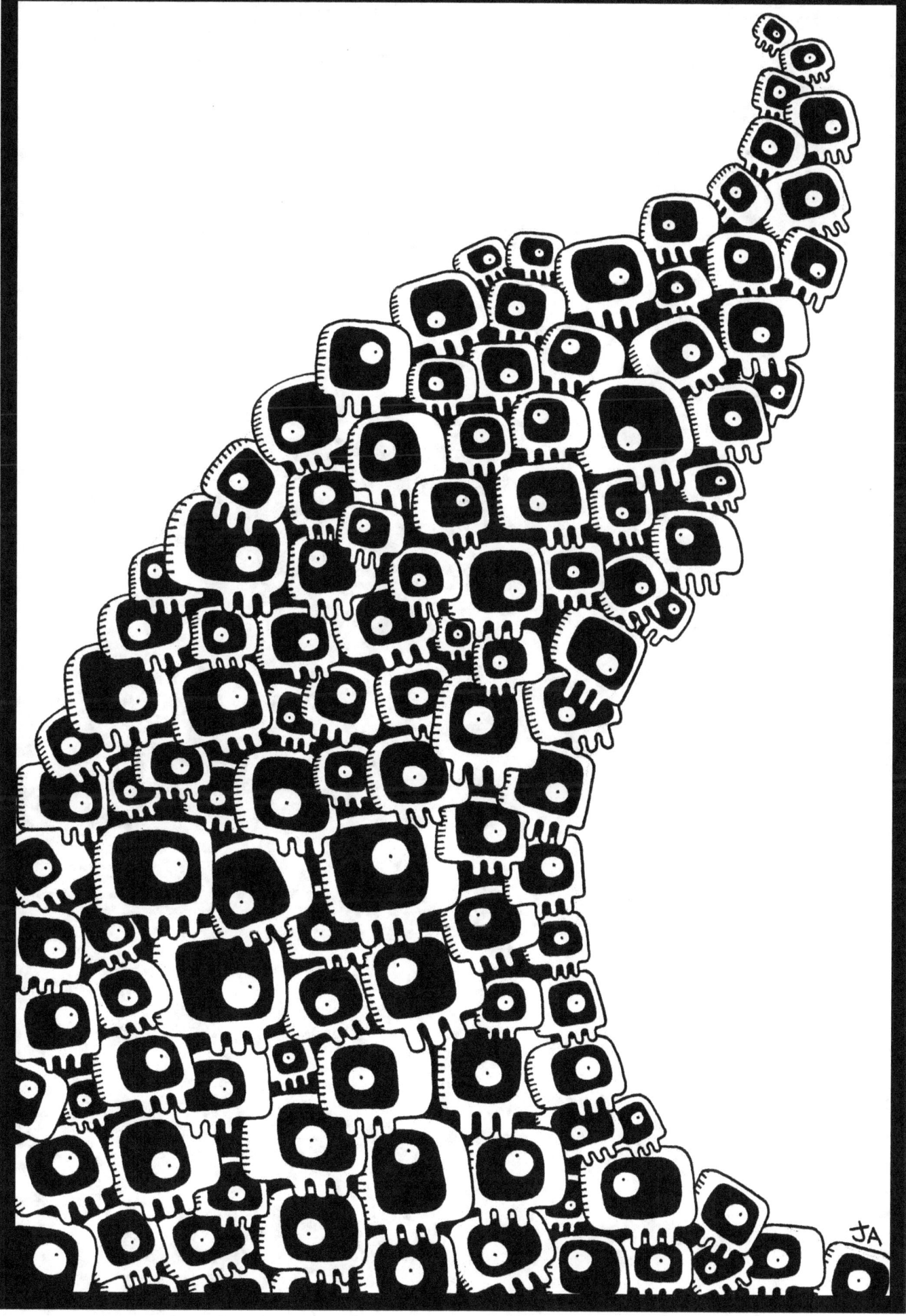

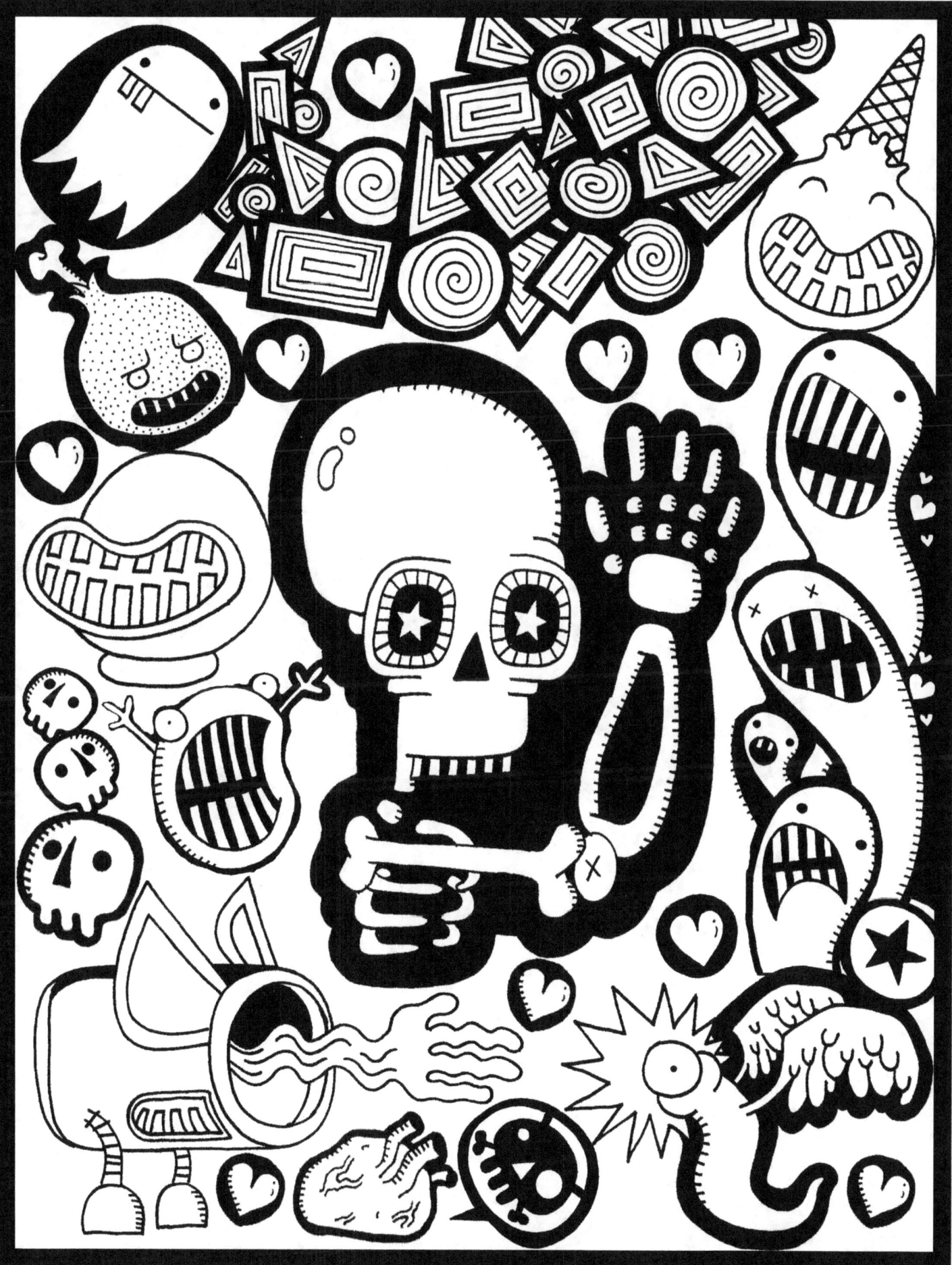

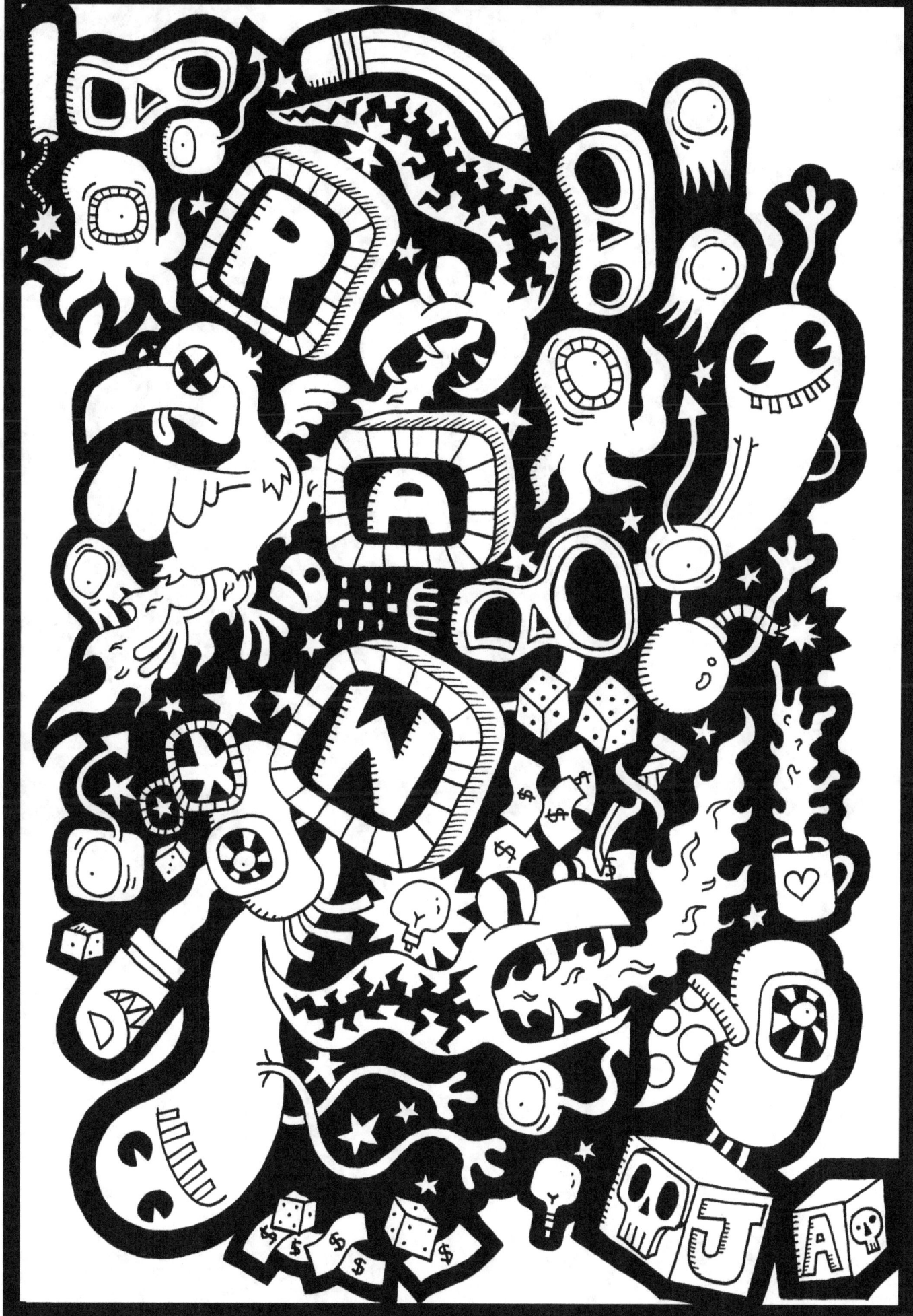

ABOUT THE AUTHOR

JAMIE ARMES IS AN INDIE
ILLUSTRATOR.

THOUGH FREQUENTLY DRAWING
SKULLS,
HE POSSESSES ONLY HIS OWN.

DESIGNED BY

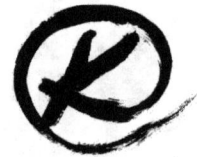

www.ingramcontent.com/pod-product-compliance
Lightning Source LLC
Chambersburg PA
CBHW081206180526
45170CB00006B/2228